12/09

D1114849

ZIPPORA KARZ

the Sugarless Plum

HARLEQUIN®

HARLEQUIN®

the SUGARLESS PLUM
ISBN-13: 978-0-373-89203-7

Copyright © 2009 by Zippora Karz

All rights reserved. The reproduction, transmission or utilization of this work in whole or in part in any form by any electronic, mechanical or other means, now known or hereafter invented, including xerography, photocopying and recording, or in any information storage or retrieval system, is forbidden without the written permission of the publisher. For permission please contact Harlequin Enterprises Limited, 225 Duncan Mill Road, Don Mills, Ontario, Canada, M3B 3K9.

The names and identifying details of some characters in this book have been changed.

Library of Congress Cataloging-in-Publication Data

Karz, Zippora.
    The sugarless plum : a ballerina's triumph over diabetes / Zippora Karz.
    p. cm.
    ISBN 978-0-373-89203-7 (hardcover)
    1. Ballet dancers—United States—Biography. 2. Diabetics—United States—Biography. I. Title.
GV1785.K36A3 2009
792.802'8092—dc22
[B]
                        2009015679

® and TM are trademarks owned and used by the trademark owner and/or its licensee. Trademarks indicated with ® are registered in the United States Patent and Trademark Office, the Canadian Trade Marks Office and/or other countries.

www.eHarlequin.com

Printed in U.S.A.

In loving memory of
my mother, Ellen,
and my grandmother, Gloria

CONTENTS

As a child, I had a recurring dream. In my dream I'm a young girl gliding across a smooth, sandy-brown, claylike surface. My eyes are unfocused as I move gracefully in a figure eight on this round space. My feet are bare, yet I move with such fluid grace that it seems as though I'm wearing skates.

My legs are long and gangly like those of a newborn colt or filly, but they have strength. There is a smile on my face as I float in a reverie on this slippery, cool, smooth clay.

Then suddenly, for no apparent reason, I start to move faster, so fast that the clay surface dries, cracks and starts to fly up around me. I'm caught in a tornado of broken clay. The chunks… me…everything…are spinning out of control. I'm about to explode when suddenly the chunks recede, time slows, and I am gliding once more in my reverie.

PART ONE

On and Off My Toes

ONE

I'm twenty-one years old. For the past three years I've been a member of the New York City Ballet, a company revered by audiences, critics and dancers.

Tonight I'm in a brand-new ballet, *Les Petits Riens,* dancing a leading role, choreographed especially for me by the company's ballet-master-in-chief, Peter Martins. The ballet's premiere performance will be given at the New York State Theater at Lincoln Center before an audience of 2,700 people.

For days I've been feeling that special, nervous anticipation that always precedes a premiere. This role is a tremendous step up in my career, an incredible honor.

Even though I'm excited, the truth is, I'm completely exhausted. Burned out. I'm trying not to complain because I figure that the other hundred dancers in the company are equally tired. We're at the end of a grueling four-month season. We've danced eight shows a week, and between performances we're taking class and rehearsing constantly.

3

I'm starting to wonder what's wrong with me. Lately, I'm always thirsty, I'm dizzy a lot, and I need to pee all the time. I've convinced myself it's because of my exhaustion, but that doesn't explain all these symptoms or account for the awful, oozing sores under my arms. They're getting worse, and the worse they get, the more they freak me out. When I raise my arms, the ripping and burning is almost intolerable, and dancers have to raise their arms a lot. I'm used to having minor irritations under my arms because, as a member of the corps de ballet, I wear a different costume every night and none of them was originally made to fit me. My shoulders are sloped, which means that the bodice is often too long and the stiff material rubs against my armpits as I dance. But the irritations have never developed into sores like the ones I have now.

Two weeks ago, during a break in rehearsals, I ran to the Urgent Care Center on West Seventy-second Street to see what I could do to get rid of the sores. The doctor there gave me a massive shot of antibiotics and sent me on my way. One week later, I had ten times the number of sores. After that, Peter Martins's secretary gave me the phone number of a dermatologist, who put me on a different antibiotic. Neither of the doctors had given me any explanation as to why they'd been getting worse instead of better.

A week later, I phoned the dermatologist to let him know the new antibiotic wasn't working. "Isn't there anything you can do to help me?" I begged. "Next week I'm dancing the most important performance of my life. I have to be able to lift my arms."

"I'm just a dermatologist," he said. "If you want more answers, you've got to get some blood work done." I didn't have time for all these doctors, and I didn't understand what was so difficult about getting those sores to heal. It never occurred to me that this was anything more than a minor—albeit unsightly and painful—problem. But if I was going to dance, I needed to lift my arms. I had to do *something.* So, with the greatest reluctance, I took his advice, went to an internist and had blood work done.

Now another week has gone by and I've put the blood test out of my mind. I've calmed down about the sores. They're still there, but I'm not feeling the pain. I'm actually more concerned with how they look than how they feel, so I've been covering them with thick layers of pancake makeup. The sores make me feel like a fraud. Ballerinas are supposed to be delicate, ethereal creatures, and in some ways I still look the part: I have large dark eyes, a small head on a long neck, a slender, elongated body and expressive feet. But these days I feel more like a toad than a princess.

Sitting at my dressing table an hour before my premier performance in *Les Riens,* I look at my hands. It doesn't surprise me that they're shaking. Luckily, the dancer at the dressing table next to mine is my younger sister Romy, who joined the company this year. Even though we look a lot alike, she is now taller than I am. We're best friends, and in a tense situation like this she always knows exactly how I feel. I know how she feels, too; she's even more nervous for me than I am for myself.

We decide that I should wear a pair of her rhinestone earrings onstage for good luck. That way she'll be with me—in a sense—when I'm dancing. This makes both of us feel better. It's time to put on my costume. It's gorgeous. Yellow silk trimmed in lace and pearls, with a tight, corset-like bodice, sleeves that come to just above the elbows, and a short, starched peplum skirt. Except for the fact that the skirt ends at the top of my thigh, it's made to look like what a lady would have worn in the time of Mozart. The only problem is that it's way too tight. My appetite is driving me crazy. I'm hungry all the time and I can't stop eating. It's got to be nerves. I hope that's all it is.

But now, with the premiere less than an hour away, I have to find a pair of pointe shoes—a perfect pair. The shoes I need tonight have to be soft enough to conform to my feet, but not too soft. I must have a pair like that somewhere, but where? I rifle through the ever-present tangle of items on my dressing room floor: worn-out tights, practice clothes, a mass of pointe shoes, some stiff and new, others danced ragged. Without the right pointe shoes, I won't be able to do the first turn of my solo; it's incredibly difficult and if it isn't perfect, my entire performance will be sunk.

The right shoes can make the difference between a good and bad performance. I put on pair after pair and try them out by rising up on the tips of my toes. At last, a pair I can use. Finally.

I lace up the shoes, crossing their pink-satin ribbons in front of my ankle. I wrap the ribbons one time around, then tie them in a tight knot toward the inside of my ankle. I look in the mirror: hair looks fine, makeup looks good.

I squeeze my false eyelashes between my thumb and index finger to make sure they'll stay glued when the sweat starts pouring.

With less than a half hour to go before the performance, I'm worn out by my own emotions: I'm jittery and excited at one moment, frozen in panic the next. I have to dance better than I've ever danced. *Les Petits Riens* is a great chance for me, but it could be my last chance if I don't keep up with the other dancers.

As a dancer, I've always been passionate and expressive. My challenge is technical strength. I'm more colt than thoroughbred, and my current physical condition is making my footwork shaky. It may be perfectly precise one moment, and then suddenly, for no apparent reason, I fall off my pointes. Dancers need to be in control of every part of their body, from their fingers to the tips of their toes. That connection is essential, and lately, I don't have it. No wonder I've lost the confidence I've struggled so hard to attain.

Confidence can make the difference between just dancing and dancing well. It's what allows a ballerina to weather the vulnerabilities of being barely clothed onstage, of risking falling down or looking ridiculous with every leap or turn. Confidence propels a performance. It allows you to manage the dichotomies that come with ballet: trying to make impossibly difficult moves look easy; having to be the embodiment of femininity as you execute steps that require an athlete's strength and stamina.

The combined loss of confidence and physical ability explains why I've been getting fewer good parts lately. It hurts to be excluded from ballets I love, especially those choreographed by

Jerome Robbins, who has singled me out in the past and given me the honor of dancing leading roles in his works.

Outside the ballet world, Robbins is best known as the director and choreographer of hit Broadway musicals like *West Side Story* and *Fiddler on the Roof*. But he would tell you that his most substantive and significant career has been with New York City Ballet. Jerry is NYCB's resident genius, the only person gifted enough to assume the mantle of George Balanchine, who was the co-founder of NYCB and generally recognized as the greatest choreographer of the twentieth century.

When Balanchine was alive, every dancer in the company had the same dream: that Mr. B, as he was known, would choose him or her to dance one of his new works. In the three years since his death, we've all come to dream of being chosen by Jerry. In my view, working with Jerry, being nurtured by his genius, would lead me on the path to realizing my dream of becoming a great dancer. This is the dream I've nurtured since I was fifteen, when I moved to New York to study at the School of American Ballet, the school that Balanchine established as a training ground for his company. It was there that I discovered the world of Balanchine, and came to dream that my dancing might make me a small part of his legacy. If I dreamed bigger, it would be to someday become a soloist, one of the rare and special dancers who are featured in leading roles, an experience that allows the ultimate freedom of expression.

It's been exactly one year since Jerry chose me to dance the role he created for the great Gelsey Kirkland in *The Goldberg Variations,* his masterpiece. At NYCB, it is customary to give big chances to young dancers. Balanchine loved to single out future stars from the corps de ballet and thrust them into the limelight. Peter Martins followed suit, and it was he who picked me, during my second year with the company, to be the Sugar Plum Fairy in *The Nutcracker.* Jerry had his eye on me, as well, and a few weeks after I danced Sugar Plum he cast me in Kirkland's role.

I put my entire being into it, and I did well.

For a time.

Minutes before the curtain goes up, the phone in the hallway rings. It's the only phone for the thirty-five female corps dancers who share a huge dressing room on the fourth floor. I don't have time to answer it, but I hear another dancer calling, "It's for you, Zippora."

Who could be calling me? Reluctantly, I head down the hall. It's the switchboard operator.

"Your doctor called again today," he says. "She said it was urgent."

Damn. She's called every day this week, sometimes twice a day. I'm rehearsing all the time and keep forgetting to call her back. What could possibly be so urgent?

It's now five minutes before the performance. The eight dancers in *Riens* are onstage. Even as the audience enters the theater we're behind the heavy curtain, still practicing, still trying to perfect intricacies of partnering and footwork. My reviews last year for *The Nutcracker* were nothing less than spectacular. In the *New York Times,* Jennifer Dunning wrote that my Sugar Plum was "a smooth blend of regal ballerina manners and the coltish classical purity of a student." In the *New York Post,* Clive Barnes hailed me as a "potential star." Now I'm on the stage with seven other potential stars. As in every company, there are more dancers than leading roles, so we're all competing for a slice of a very small pie.

"What's the matter?" one of the dancers asks me.

"I can hardly breathe," I say. "My costume's too tight."

Another dancer overhears me. "Oh, really?" she says, "Mine's too loose."

You bitch, I think, but say nothing.

Moments before the performance begins, I give my partner, Peter Boal, a quick hug. *"Merde,"* all eight of us call out to one another, our voices overlapping. *Merde* means "shit" in French. Before a show, it's our way of saying "break a leg" or "good luck."

It's bad luck to say "thank you." Dancers are nothing if not superstitious. If someone tells you *"Merde,"* you just smile and say *"Merde"* back.

The stage manager calls out, "Dancers, stand by." The house lights dim. The excited murmuring of the audience gives way to silence. For the next few moments there will be darkness both in the house, where the audience sits waiting, and on the stage, where the dancers are poised to begin. I take my pose. Slowly, inexorably, the heavy curtain rises. Suddenly, the stage is bathed in light. I feel a chill as cold air from the house washes over me. I look at the conductor. He raises his baton. When the baton sweeps downward the orchestra explodes in sound as the Mozart score begins.

We start to move. I think about how much I love dancing with my peers. Once a performance starts, all feelings of competition are set aside. I love the secret looks we give one another; I love the way we urge one another on with our eyes. The opening section finishes. I'm breathing heavily as I bow to the audience. Six dancers leave the stage. Only Peter and I remain to dance a pas de deux, followed by our solos.

The stage is eerily silent as I walk across it, soundless in my pointe shoes. I take my pose opposite Peter. The audience is hushed, expectant. The music begins softly. It is sweet, loving, innocent. I love this music, I love these steps, I love the way Peter and I play together onstage. Too soon, it ends. We bow; the audience applauds.

I run offstage utterly exhausted. Mercifully, Peter's solo is first.

While he's onstage, I'm supposed to be resting, but that's out of the question. My solo comes next and I'm totally intimidated by the very first step, that incredibly difficult turn—harder than any turn I've ever had to do—that turn for which I needed the perfect pair of shoes. When Peter Martins choreographed that turn, he and I were both shocked at how perfectly I did it the very first time out. But it was a fluke, and every day since then I've had to re-create that fluke in rehearsals. Tonight I have to nail it. I take a practice turn and fall off my toe. Now I'm terrified.

Suddenly Jerome Robbins appears backstage. He steps out of the darkness into the first wing, the very place from which Balanchine used to watch every performance. I shouldn't notice. I'm supposed to be focused on my steps. But all I can think of is how he replaced me with a younger dancer in *The Goldberg Variations.*

Jerry has an animal-like sixth sense. He can smell fear, and even if he likes you, your fear can drive him crazy or drive him away. He's remote, grand, known to be cruel. And he's known for his temper. I want him to see me dance. I want him to love me. I want him to ask me to dance *Goldberg* again.

Onstage, Peter finishes his solo with a flourish. Backstage, we hear the explosive applause. It trails off. Now it's my turn to dance. I run onto the stage and stand in fifth position. I watch the conductor. His hand goes up, then comes down. The music starts and I begin. I sail around on my toe. I don't fall off. Amazing. It's as if all the years of training have been preparing me for this single moment.

After one revolution, I slow my momentum to a full stop. Still on pointe, I balance on my left toe while my right leg extends to the side. Then I bend my left knee, as my right leg bends and comes to rest behind my ankle in the position called *coupe.* I have never done it so perfectly. "Don't relax yet, you have to do it one more time," I tell myself. The second turn goes just as well. Now I am free to dance my heart out.

I chassé and bourrée all over the stage. It's as if I'm skipping through a meadow on a sunny day. Jerry has to see my talent. He has to love me again. Still, while Jerry chose me for my dancing, I realize that something else drew him, as well. After all, everyone at City Ballet can dance. Everyone is special. Everyone sparkles.

But what Jerry saw in me was an extra sparkle. Maybe it's not possible to shine when your body is struggling as mine is.

Have I lost my sparkle in his eyes?

At the end of my solo I have a series of turns on the diagonal. I'm supposed to end up right at the wing where Jerry's standing. I run across the stage. Just as I begin turning toward him, I see him walking away while I'm still dancing. I'm performing for more than two thousand people, but the only one I can think of is Jerry. I'm smiling for the audience, but my heart is sinking.

I try not to think about Jerry as I take my curtain call with the rest of the cast to enthusiastic applause.

An hour later, the stage is bare, the audience has long since gone home, and I'm leaving the theater with Romy, cradling a bouquet of roses from Peter Martins. As we're walking out, I notice a message tacked to the bulletin board: "Zippora, urgent. Call your doctor."

I know I should call her, and I promise myself that I will—just as soon as the season is over, which is in just three weeks. I get through the remaining five performances of *Les Petits Riens* on sheer strength of will. But a few days later I receive an unexpected wake-up call in the form of a dream.

I've always believed in the significance of dreams, and this one is particularly frightening. I dream that I'm in a car. The car isn't moving and the windows and the doors are open, but the engine is running. Suddenly, the windows roll up and the doors lock shut. Then the fumes from the exhaust start coming through the vents in the dashboard and filling the car. I can't breathe and I can't get out. I wake up just before I suffocate.

As I lie there, trying to catch my breath, the dream seems to me like a portent. The car is my body and the exhaust is something happening inside me that is life-threatening. I realize that something is not right.

That afternoon I phone the doctor during a five-minute rehearsal break, and she tells me I have to come in immediately. A few hours later, I'm in her waiting room. It's cold and sterile. It gives me the creeps. It's six-twenty and I've been waiting for an hour. To get there, I had to skip my final rehearsal of the day for a ballet I was scheduled to dance the following week. Now I have to get back to the theater by seven-thirty to put on my makeup and get ready for this evening's performance. I don't have time to sit here, but I need to know what's so urgent and she wouldn't tell me over the phone.

Finally, the door to her office opens. She invites me in. She's a tall, thin, attractive woman in a tailored white doctor's coat. She's smiling, but I see pity in that smile and it puts me on edge. She looks as if she's about to tell me she ran over my dog. She studies my chart for a moment, then tells me that my blood sugar levels are 350. Normal levels, she says, are 120 or under. I ask what this means. She says it means that I have diabetes.

Diabetes? I've heard of it. It's one of those charity diseases, the kind they raise money for. She hands me four pamphlets that describe what may happen to me: heart disease, stroke, blindness, kidney failure, foot and/or leg amputations.

I can't take it in. I refuse to take it in. Instead, I try to figure out how long it will take me to get back to the theater. If I get out of here soon I can make it. Even if I don't get a cab, I can walk it in twenty minutes.

She says we can discuss a treatment plan during our next appointment. Another appointment? Why can't we discuss it now? I want to know what to do. I want everything to go back to being the way it was. But all she will say is that she doesn't want me to feel deprived of food; that feeling deprived could cause me to go overboard eating the wrong thing. She says it's not okay to eat a whole cake—as if I don't know that—but it's all right to have a little piece of cake. What is she talking about? I'm a dancer. I'm disciplined. I wouldn't eat a bite of cake if I'm not supposed to. Anyway, I don't eat cake. Period.

I hate this doctor. She's talking to me as if I'm a child or an idiot or both. I don't trust her. She has no idea whom she's dealing with. She doesn't know me. I'm in her office no more than fifteen minutes, and I'm so turned off by her condescending attitude that I don't even bother to make another appointment.

Finally, I get back to the theater. Now I can focus on the ballet I'm dancing tonight, Balanchine's *Piano Concerto No. 2*. For dancers in the corps it's one of the most demanding ballets. Even the strongest corps dancers have problems getting through it.

The section that worries me most comes in the third movement. It's tired me so much in rehearsal that I've wanted to run off stage and fall to the ground in an exhausted heap. Instead, I have to execute one of the most difficult and controlled sequences of steps. How I am going to manage it, especially now? Losing limbs…. going blind…I hate that doctor's voice. I want it out of my head.

As terrified as I am to dance tonight, I need the stage right now. Onstage, I feel alive. I feel safe. What happens onstage isn't real, of course, but it's where I can enact, experience and connect to the grandest human emotions, from exultation to despair. In that sense, being on-stage often feels more real and immediate than life.

There are just twenty minutes until the performance, and I have to warm up my muscles. But the more I try to get warm, the colder and clammier I feel. Backstage, I put resin on the heels of my tights and the heels of my pointe shoes so they won't slip off. Next to the resin box there's a big bucket of water. I've dipped my heels in this water hundreds of times to keep my shoes from coming off. Now I can't. The water's too cold. I'm too cold.

I've got to calm down.

I sit in a corner and, as dancers do before a performance, take a few minutes to sew my toe shoe ribbons together so they don't unravel. The wardrobe mistress helps me hook up my costume. I look in the mirror to make sure the picture is complete: costume, shoes, hair, makeup.

"Dancers, the call is onstage," says the stage manager, his voice booming through the loudspeaker. Oh, no. I have to pee! How is this possible? I went to the bathroom less than half an hour ago. But I have to go again. And I really have to, because when you need to pee there's no way you can dance for thirty-five minutes.

I have just a few minutes until the overture starts. I race to the bathroom closest to the stage followed by the wardrobe lady, who has to unhook my entire costume and then hook it all back up again.

Thank God the overture for Tchaikovsky's Piano Concerto No. 2 is long. The orchestra will play for several minutes before the curtain is raised. I'm back onstage, going over the sequence that has me so worried. I do it over and over, reminding myself to hold my stomach tight. The overture becomes louder, stronger, fiercer.

Three more minutes until the curtain goes up. I take my place. I love dancing to Tchaikovsky's music. It's passionate and bold. It always awakens my deepest feelings.

Suddenly, I begin to shake. To my horror, I start to cry. I try to stop, but I can't. I hate public displays of emotion. I don't cry easily, but I can't help crying now. One of the male dancers hurries over and puts his arm around me. He asks what's wrong. I'm sobbing uncontrollably as other dancers gather around me. I have to pull myself together. I need to lighten the tension. "It's a good thing my makeup is waterproof," I say. The others exchange looks.

I know what they're thinking, "Why is she freaking out?"

I wipe my cheeks and pinch my false lashes to be sure they've weathered the storm. The curtain rises. The ballet begins with a line of eight corps de ballet women positioned in a diagonal line facing the audience. We wear blue costumes with flowing chiffon skirts and sparkles across the neckline. Facing us are eight corps de ballet men. Their backs are slightly to the audience. The music becomes gentle and soft. The men walk toward the ladies.

The dancing begins. Tears flow down my cheeks throughout the entire performance.

As I dance, my mind is racing…losing limbs, kidney failure, heart disease, stroke, going blind.

I just need rest, I tell myself, and my blood sugar levels will go back to normal. The long winter season has been too demanding. It'll be over in two weeks. Then I'll have three weeks to recover before the spring season begins. Anyway, I'll bet the diagnosis is just a lab error. There's no way I can have diabetes. I'm a twenty-one-year-old dancer with the New York City Ballet. Things like that don't happen to people like me.

TWO

Although I'm still determined to get through the end of the season, once I receive my diagnosis it becomes harder to ignore the physical symptoms that have been plaguing me for so long. I'm constantly licking my lips, which are painfully dry. No matter how much water I drink, I'm always thirsty. I can't wind down, and I'm barely sleeping, which is probably why I'm spacey all the time.

But at nine-thirty the morning after my doctor visit and my onstage meltdown, I have to ignore how I feel and get myself to company class as I do every day. No matter how accomplished a dancer becomes, we never stop taking class, and we're expected to be there on time. As I hurry down the hallway, I hear piano music in the distance. Class has begun. This is the first time I've ever been late.

I sneak in between two dancers at the front barre. Holding the barre with my left hand, I join in the morning ritual. It begins with pliés: in a plié you bend your legs, slowly lowering yourself nearly to the floor, and then rise up again while keeping your back straight and your knees over your toes, which ensures a turned-out position. We practice pliés using four of the five positions of the feet in ballet. There's also a third position, but it's never used; in fact, Balanchine hated third position. He thought it was ugly.

I look at Suzanne Farrell at the barre across from me. The best-known Balanchine ballerina of her time, she was also his greatest muse.

Suzanne is my favorite ballerina. Today she is serene as always, wearing her signature Spanish-style shawl, which is brilliantly colored in deep blue, red, green and orange. She wears the shawl wrapped and tied at her breastbone; it flows with every motion of her body.

I've always been flattered that Suzanne seems to notice me. Now, in class, I pray she doesn't look my way. When barre ends, I rush to the bathroom. In the six hours of rehearsals that follow, I'll be in and out of that bathroom again and again. Somehow I make it through the day. The toughest part will be getting through this evening's performance.

I can't let myself think about how bad I feel. I have to keep pushing. Before putting on my makeup, I wait in line to see the physical therapist, hoping to gain some relief from the piercing pain in my muscles. A dancer's muscles are always sore, but the pain that I am experiencing has become excruciating and I have no idea why.

The physical therapy room is small, a space maybe ten-by-ten feet that houses a physical therapist, a massage therapist, two massage tables and machines for ultrasound and electrical stimulation. The therapists are available three hours before each performance. They're needed because every dancer is always in some kind of pain: a torn calf muscle, a back in spasm, a recovering foot fracture, an arthritic hip. We all dance injured, and we all operate on the assumption that if we can walk, we can dance.

In the therapy room, I avoid making eye contact with the other dancers. When I'm trying to stay calm, I've always found that it's best to keep to myself. Now one of the women in the corps approaches me and rests her hand on my shoulder. "I know what you're going through," she says. "I have an uncle who has diabetes."

Everyone in the room looks up. Then they look at me. My face turns red with rage. I want to scream. I want to slap her.

How could she know? I haven't told anybody. Not even my own sister.

"I saw the same doctor yesterday," the dancer continues, anticipating my question. "She mentioned it to me."

I shoot her a look that says, "Not one more word or it's a fist in your face."

Then it hits me: Everyone in the company sees that doctor. And she's talking about me. I feel betrayed, helpless. How dare she say anything about me to anybody?

Oh, well, I tell myself. So what? It doesn't matter. I'm going to prove that stupid doctor is wrong, anyway. I don't have diabetes. I just need to rest.

I run to the bathroom again.

* * *

Three hours later I'm onstage performing. My legs are shaking so much I'm afraid they're going to give out on me. I can't feel my toes. I'm cold and clammy and falling off pointe on every step. I'm dizzy. I feel like I'm going to pass out.

I have to pull it together. I can't fail, especially not in front of Peter Martins. Even though I danced well in *Les Petits Riens,* a dancer's career is all about consistency. If Peter doesn't feel that he can depend on me, he'll never let me dance a leading role again. I hear the doctor's voice in my head again, "You have a disease called diabetes." I have to banish that voice. I focus on the dancing as hard as I can.

When I'm finally walking down the hallway to my apartment that night, I sigh with relief. Not a moment later I feel like I'm going to faint. The dizziness, the hunger, the urination, the sores, the thirst—the more I try to push, the more I'm falling apart. I lie in bed staring at the ceiling.

There are just two weeks to go in the season now, but I don't think I can make it. I've had physical problems before, numerous foot and ankle injuries, but I could always push through them. In fact, I'd had a broken fourth metatarsal in my foot when I danced a lead in one of Balanchine's ballets that inspired him when I was just a student to be interested in me for the company. My doctor couldn't believe I was walking, let alone dancing.

Why is it different now? Why can't I hold on? My usual reserve of determination is gone, replaced by constant brain fog. And for the first time I have to admit that maybe there really is something wrong with me.

I almost pass out again as I get up to go to the bathroom. Looking at my pale reflection in the mirror, so different from the one I presented onstage just hours before, I finally face the fact that I'm not well. I cannot continue dancing.

Before company class the next morning, I go over to Rosemary Dunleavy, the main ballet mistress for members of the corps de ballet and the person who has the power to determine which corps members will dance what and when. She was once a City Ballet corps dancer herself, although she doesn't look much like a ballerina: She's five foot four with hair so short she never needs a bun. She wears baggy sweats and a large knit sweater that hangs halfway down her thighs. She never lets anyone see her body, even though she's thinner than most dancers. I know this because she changes her clothes in the same bathroom on the fifth floor that I'm always using these days.

Rosemary is the only ballet mistress who takes class with us. During the rehearsal day, when she teaches us choreography, she wears her pointe shoes and demonstrates the steps as if she were performing onstage. Class is as important to her as it is to me. As a young company member I spend most of my day in the studio with her. She's yet another extremely important person whom I very much want to like me.

I'm terrified now as I kneel at her side while she lies on the floor, stretching her leg over her head. "I'm not feeling well," I say. "I don't think I can perform right now."

Rosemary's owl-like eyes get bigger. "What's wrong? Are you okay?"

What do I say? If you pull out the day of a performance, you'd better have a great reason, a big one. I have a big one, but I also don't want her to think I have a problem. I can't let *myself* think I have a problem. "I just found out that I have diabetes. I need to learn what to do for it. I think I should go home for a while." I can't believe I've actually said that. Going home is the right thing to do, but it hadn't crossed my mind until the words were out of my mouth.

Only now does it strike me that this is a pivotal moment in my life.

Rosemary stares at me as her mind races to figure out what ballets are going to be performed that evening and what parts I have in them. "What about *Coppelia?*" she asks. "Can't you do it?" I'm supposed to dance as one of Coppelia's friends that night. It's a great part, with dancing in all three acts, and I love it.

I desperately want to say "Yes, I can do it." Instead I say, "I'm sorry, I just can't." Rosemary looks away. I'm already out of her mind. She's moved on to deciding which dancer will replace me. I pick up my dance bag and leave the studio.

Right now, only two things matter:

I've got to get some help.

I've got to get out of there.

PART TWO

Portrait of a Young Dancer

THREE

To understand why it was so difficult for me to tell Rosemary that I would have to miss not just one performance but the last two weeks of the season, you have to first understand how central ballet had become to my life.

By this point all I wanted was to be at the theater and dancing all the time. Even though I hadn't been one of those little girls who dreams of becoming a ballerina, there was a confluence of circumstances leading me, without my even being aware of it, in that direction. I had been exposed to dance at a very early age, and my mother, who had also been a dancer, had found me a truly inspiring teacher. Dancing was, quite literally, in my blood.

The first dancer in the family was my mother's mother, my grandma Gloria. As a little girl, it had been Gloria's job to take her younger sister, Priscilla, to ballet class, wait until the lesson was over and take her back home. Priscilla had been stricken with polio, and her doctor thought that ballet lessons would be good therapy for her legs. But Priscilla refused to get up, much less dance. Day after day, as the instructor tried to coax Priscilla to participate, my grandmother sat on the sidelines moving her feet to the music. Finally, the increasingly frustrated teacher noticed her sitting there and said, "You look like you would like to dance," which was all the encouragement Gloria needed. She got up and kicked her leg above her head. "You're the dancer!" the teacher exclaimed, and so a career was born.

By the time she was twelve, Grandma had performed her solo routine of high kicks and acrobatics for President Coolidge. At thirteen, she was under contract with the William Morris Agency. Five years after that, she was performing with a touring company. Jack Levand, a handsome high school senior, was working at night as an usher in the theater. One night he watched her performance and fell madly in love. He pursued Gloria for a year, following her around the country, and when they were both nineteen, they eloped. Grandma continued performing in vaudeville and Broadway shows until Jack finished college at Ohio State University and they started a family. But even then she couldn't give up the stage, so she created an act she could perform with her two young daughters. My mother, Ellen, was just three years old when she began to appear onstage with her older sister, Arlene, and their mother.

In due course my mother was accepted at the renowned Juilliard School of Music in New York City, where she majored in modern dance. But she was convinced that she would never dance professionally, both because she lacked the confidence and drive it would take to compete and because—even though she had been dancing her entire life—she had started her formal training so late. While she was at Juilliard she read an article about George Balanchine's fourth wife, Tanaquil Le Clercq, whom he had discovered when she was just twelve. When Tanaquil was fifteen, Balanchine asked her to dance with him in a piece he had choreographed for a March of Dimes benefit. In the ballet Balanchine danced the part of the evil Polio and she danced the part of his young victim who ultimately recovers. In a terrible twist of fate, Tanaquil—who had by then become one of Balanchine's great ballerinas and his wife—was stricken with polio at the age of twenty-seven. Balanchine believed that she, too, would recover just as her character had in the ballet. Sadly, however, the real Tanaquil was confined to a wheelchair for the rest of her life.

My mother was so moved by this story that she decided to become a physical therapist. But dance continued to be part of her life, and she continued to perform and teach traditional folk dancing, just as my grandmother continued to choreograph and dance.

My own introduction to dance occurred, of all places, in Thailand. I was born in 1965, the second of four children my mother was to have in the space of five years. My parents named me after my father's mother, Celia, whose Hebrew name was Tsiporah, which means "little bird."

Michele, my older sister, was the leader as well as the most mischievous, and the one who could always make us laugh. Gary, who came after me, and my younger sister, Romy, were generally good kids. I was good, too, but I was the most difficult and demanding of the four. With less than two years between my birth and my brother's, Mom didn't have as much time as she would have liked to spend with me. Perhaps that's the reason why I was such a needy child. I always seemed to have more energy than I knew what to do with, and my emotions often flew out of control, as if I'd been plugged into some kind of electrical socket. I might be calm one minute and crying uncontrollably or having a temper tantrum the next.

My moods were a family affair, and the family joke was that, as the only Gemini, I had a split personality. I can still remember our visits to my mother's parents. My grandpa Jack would open the door and everyone else would run inside while he quickly shut the door, leaving me outside by myself. Then, from behind the closed door, he would call out in a cheery voice, "Are you the good Zippora or (changing his tone to one full of doom and gloom) the bad Zippora?"

No matter how happy I'd been on the ride over, the pressure of having to be good—and the assumption that I wouldn't be— always set me off. "I'm the bad Zippora," I'd yell out, running to the shelter of the kumquat trees lining my grandparents' front yard. Talking silently to those trees, I imagined how one of those kumquats would feel if someone bit into its sour fruit, mistaking it for a sweet, juicy orange or tangerine, and then spit it out in disgust as soon as they tasted its astringent flavor. That was how I generally felt—misunderstood. And then, once I'd calmed down, I'd wander inside to join the rest of the group and the whole incident would be forgotten—as if it had never happened.

Although I adored my grandpa Jack, his old-school way of dealing with my emotional volatility wasn't what I needed. Over the years I came to understand that he was simply trying to motivate me to behave better in the only way he knew how, but the kind of kid I was simply didn't respond well to that kind of treatment. I did much better when left to my own devices to reach my own conclusions. My mother understood this, and even though she didn't always have time for me, she always gave me the freedom to be exactly who I was.

Eventually, it was through dance that I found something I really liked about myself and, in addition, a way to release my excess energy and the discipline to direct that energy into something positive. But all that was still in the future. In 1969, at the height of the Vietnam War, my father, a cardiologist, was drafted and assigned to Fort Carson in Colorado. A year later he volunteered to go to Thailand, so, when I was five, the entire family moved to Bangkok.

Even at that age I was keenly aware of how different this place was from our home in the San Fernando Valley of Los Angeles. I remember turning on the bathroom faucet and waiting while black water streamed out for several minutes before turning clear. I remember watching my mother rinse all our vegetables in Clorox before preparing them. I remember the mosquito netting around our beds, canoe trips with my family down the Chao Phraya River, and watching the Thai people wash their clothes in that dirty water, where they also swam and bathed, and which they also drank.

What I remember most, however, is the magic of Thailand—the glorious colors, the costumes, the music, the scents and, most of all, the dance.

My mother, Michele, and I took Thai dance lessons. Most of the movements involved the head and arms, with our knees bending here and there and maybe a step or two in either direction. I loved watching my mom as she flexed her wrists and tilted her head. Her movements were subtle and simple, but she looked beautiful as she did them, and I got to see and know her in a way I never had before.

Our teacher was a lovely, dark-haired woman with a beautiful, sweet smile, and when it was Michele's and my turn to dance, she motioned us to the center of the floor with long brass fingernails that curved outward and ended in sharp, pointed tips. She didn't speak a word of English but silently demonstrated the movements she wanted us to perform.

I remember trying to time my movements with hers, all the while staring at those fingernails. More than anything, I wanted a set just like them. My mom said I was too young to wear them during our lessons, but she did buy a set for Michele and me to share on special occasions.

There were many evenings when we put on a talent show in the living room of our apartment on the army base. On those occasions I got to wear the brass fingernails, and Michele and I wore the beautiful Thai silk dresses our mother had tailor-made for us. I loved the way I felt in my Thai costume and those fingernails, being able to remember the intricate sequences, turning my head in just the right way at the exact moment my hands moved in one pattern and my legs in another. I was just as mesmerized doing those movements as I had been watching them. Although I didn't know it at the time, I was beginning to experience the transformative power of dance.

FOUR

After a year and a half in Thailand, my father's tour of duty was over, and we returned to California. My mother asked Michele and me if we wanted to take ballet lessons, and since Michele said yes, I did, too, without thinking much about it. I just wanted to do whatever she did. At the time, if you'd asked me what I wanted to be when I grew up, I'd have said a veterinarian or a teacher of handicapped children. My idols back then were Dr. Doolittle and Helen Keller. I didn't even know that ballet was something you could do to earn a living. The one ballet I had ever seen was a "story" ballet on television, and I wasn't impressed. The dancers looked like zombies wearing too much makeup and pained expressions on their faces; their exaggerated gestures and facial expressions made no sense to me, and the performance itself was static. They were doing very little dancing, and I didn't understand why anyone would want to stand on the tips of their toes like that. The whole thing struck me as just plain stupid.

Nevertheless, if Michele was going to take lessons, I would, too.

We were in the youngest class, which included girls aged seven to nine, and at seven, I was one of the youngest. There were barres attached to the walls of the studio, which were lined with full-length mirrors. Holding on to the barre with one hand, we practiced standing with our legs and feet pointed to either side, which seemed utterly unnatural to me. Learning all those positions and steps with funny-sounding French names like plié, *tendu, dégagé, rond de jambe,* pirouette, *sauté* and grand jeté was difficult and boring. I would rather have been outside playing with my friends or spending time with my animals, but as long as I was there I wanted to do those steps at least as well as Michele.

I stuck it out for almost two years before I finally begged my mother to let me quit. I was so persistent about it that she finally agreed, providing I finish the year for which she'd already paid.

Between work and taking care of four kids, as well as a menagerie of animals that included three dogs, more cats than we could count on our fingers, turtles, sea horses and my ant farm, Mom had her hands full and was often late picking us up from class. While I was waiting, I got in the habit of going over to the window that opened into the main studio and watching the older girls take class from the school's primary teacher and co-owner of the studio, Sheila Rozann, who taught students starting in their third year and through the highest level. I'd never seen anyone exude as much energy as Sheila did, showing her students with her own body what she wanted them to do. What the advanced students were doing in that class seemed utterly different from what I'd seen on television and what I'd been struggling with as a beginner. It wasn't about emoting or telling a story; it was all about pure movement and energy.

Even though the sweat was pouring off their bodies, when they danced they looked like magical spirits, and I was entranced. Something wonderful was happening in that classroom, and I wanted to know what it was. Since I knew that the following year, when I'd move to the third level, Sheila would be my teacher, I decided that I wasn't going to quit after all.

As a young girl, Sheila had dreamed of becoming a ballerina, and everything about her body said that she should have succeeded. She was five seven, with a thin torso and long legs. She held her chest up and her shoulders back, and she walked with her feet turned out. There was just one problem: Sheila had flat feet with no instep, and without an arch she would never stand gracefully *en pointe.* She could have been a character dancer and was even offered a contract by the Ballet Russe de Monte Carlo, but to Sheila that wasn't "ballet."

Instead, she opened her own ballet school, where her teaching style was inspired by photographs of her favorite ballerinas, every one of whom turned out to have danced for George Balanchine's company, the New York City Ballet.

Just five years after she opened the school, Balanchine found her. At that time he was bringing his company to Los Angeles once a year to dance at the Greek Theatre, and they always hired local students to dance children's roles in their productions. Sheila always sent students to audition, and when one group of girls returned for a second year, it seems that Janet Reed, Balanchine's ballet mistress at the time, was so impressed with their progress that she asked them where they studied. Janet took Sheila to lunch and mentioned that she was going to tell Balanchine about her. Not long after that, Sheila got a call saying that Mr. Balanchine himself would be coming to the school to watch her teach. What he saw impressed him so much that he gave her a private lesson right on the spot, demonstrating how he liked his dancers to hold their arms and fingers and showing her how to do a proper *tendu*. But then he said, "You know I can't use you because you have no feet." Sheila, of course, had never even thought that he thought she was auditioning for the City Ballet, but she was thrilled when he gave her an open invitation to attend his seminars and to watch classes at the School of American Ballet (SAB), which he had founded with Lincoln Kirstein, a brilliant, iconoclastic patron of the arts, as a feeder school for their company. To Balanchine, training was of crucial importance, and he modeled his ballet school on the storied Imperial School of Ballet he had attended in Russia, where standards were so high that they were regarded as equal to those of Russia's military and naval academies. That was the start of a forty-year relationship between Sheila and SAB.

Dance in Sheila's class was all about the energy that went into each step, the line of the leg, embodying the music and letting it all flow through you. Still, the technical aspects of ballet did not come easily for me. I couldn't help comparing myself to

Michele, who was two years older, and surpassed me both in strength and flexibility. Movements I was still struggling to master seemed to come easily to her. In a port de bras forward, for example, your legs are kept straight and in a turned-out position while you hold on to the barre with one hand and touch the floor with the other. Michele could put her whole hand on the floor and touch her head to her kneecaps, while I couldn't touch the floor at all. I wanted to do what she could do, but more than that, I wanted to know what it felt like to do it.

Finally, I asked my mother for help, and she showed me a hamstring stretch that she used with her physical therapy patients. I practiced that stretch over and over until, after several months, it happened—I could touch the floor with straight legs. I was only ten years old at the time, but that was probably the beginning of the determination and work ethic that would serve me well not only in my dancing career but also in the management of my illness. I had learned a profound lesson: if I focused hard on accomplishing something and worked diligently, I would eventually be able to do it well. I was learning how to transform my body into an instrument. No matter my mood, when I entered that studio I could channel my troublesome surges of energy in an entirely different way.

Most important of all, when I got my head out of the way and let the music flow through my body, I felt something bigger, grander, purer and more meaningful than anything I had ever experienced at any other time in my life.

FIVE

Aside from the dancing itself, I loved the sense of order and control I experienced in the studio because life at home had become chaotic. There I had no control at all.

I was nine years old when my parents decided to get a divorce. No one ever told us what was happening, so I couldn't understand why my mother was so angry, why my father seemed so confused and was sleeping on the couch, or why they weren't speaking to each other. Then one day my father moved out and into a one-bedroom apartment where all four of us kids often spent weekends camped on the recliner, two or three chairs pushed together, as well as the kitchen and living room floors. I remember trying very hard to rein in my emotions and not do anything that would upset them further or add to their problems. I just wanted to make things better, but this was one situation over whose outcome I didn't really have any control.

It wasn't until many years later that my mother told me they had never really learned how to communicate their needs to each other. I believe now that there was never any one precipitating event, but that my mother was simply harboring a lot of resentments they'd never discussed. By the time my father was aware of it, it was too late.

After the divorce, my mother went back to work full time and we became latchkey kids. We returned from school every day to a house that was empty except for our animals. Needless to say, the house was a mess, and so were our lives. No matter how much newspaper we put down, we'd wake up in the morning to discover that the dogs had relieved themselves all over the rug. We did our best to keep things clean, but we were just kids, and Mom invariably came home to find the sofa stripped of its cushions and the four of us hiding in the "fort" that we'd made. "Jeez Louise," she'd scream as she walked through the door. "You kids are driving me crazy!" But she never punished us. I think that because she had been brought up so strictly she never wanted to put the same kinds of restrictions on us, but she was exhausted and overwhelmed, and she just wished we'd work with her to create some kind of order in our lives.

Much as I loved playing with my sisters and brother, and was certainly part of the mess, I hated seeing my mom so unhappy and I wanted her to be okay. As a result, I began taking it upon myself to create order out of the chaos. I became hyper-responsible and began ordering my siblings around, constantly telling them to pick things up and clean up after themselves—to the point where they started to respond by saying "Yes, Mom" or "Yes, boss." Because I felt such a profound sense of responsibility for alleviating my mother's stress, I hated it when the others seemed reluctant to get with the program. I could understand why they might resent obeying my orders, but that didn't stop me from issuing them. In truth, the chaos was getting to me, too, and bossing around my brother and sisters was just my way of exerting some modicum of control.

Besides the pleasure I found in my classes with Sheila, the one activity that gave the whole family a bit of happiness and a break from our never-ending squabbles was horseback riding. Ever since she was a little girl, riding had been my mother's greatest love, and now it was something we could all do together. Being on horseback and being in the studio were the two places where I felt happy and that I belonged.

That said, however, accidents happen. One day when we took a trail that went around the golf course near the stable, the horse I was on got hit in the foot by a golf ball, which caused him to buck and rear, throwing me off his back and into the air. I landed on my ankle, spraining it badly. For some reason the doctor I went to put me in a cast and I was unable to dance for the rest of the summer. When the cast finally came off, the arch on my right foot had flattened out and the foot had stiffened up so that I would never again be able to point it as well as my left. That foot would give me trouble for the rest of my dancing life.

My favorite pony was Gent, a chestnut with a black mane and tail and white spots on his back that gave away the tiny bit of Appaloosa in his gene pool. He stood just under fourteen hands, which made him a quarter inch short of being a horse. He was calm and sweet, as befitted his full name, Sir Gentleman. I had ridden many horses, but none as special as Gent. After we had been paying for our rides for a couple of years, the owners of the stable offered to sell us our favorite horses for a price so ridiculously low that even we could afford them. I bought Gent for the $150 in allowance money I'd been stashing away in a teddy-bear-shaped bank for two years.

What I didn't realize was that the reason Gent was so calm was that as a stable horse he was being ridden every day. I rode him only a few hours on weekends, and he wasn't used to being cooped up in his stall for such long stretches of time. While his gallop was still magical, his boundless energy was more than my tiny frame could handle. Heading out, he was as calm as ever, but the minute we turned back toward the stable he was transformed into a demon. No matter how hard I pulled back on the reins, within seconds he'd be flying so fast that all I could do was squeeze my legs hard and cling to his neck for dear life. As it turned out, Gent's temperament was as wild as my own; we were made for each other.

Eventually we moved our horses to the ranch owned by my mother's younger sister, Rhonda, and her husband, Michael. This was a great move for two reasons. First, because the ranch was much closer to home, so we could ride more often. And second, because Rhonda and Michael were my favorite relatives and they, in turn, thought I was really cool. In fact, they enjoyed my company so much that they'd call my mother and ask if I could come and stay for the weekend. Children of the sixties, they had lava lamps, beanbag pillows and tarot cards, and they'd named their infant daughter Raynbow. Unlike my uncommunicative parents, they demonstrated their fondness for me and for each other and I could talk to them for hours about esoteric things like past-life experiences, out-of-body experiences and UFOs. We read tarot cards together, and Michael even did faith healing with a laying-on of hands. Secretly, I wished that they could be my parents.

SIX

As time went on, ballet became the most important part of my life. I had friends in the neighborhood and I was working hard in school, but I was also spending more and more time at the studio either taking a class or waiting for the next one to begin.

Each January, ballet schools around the country sent representatives to audition students for their summer programs. When I was thirteen, Sheila decided I was old enough to try out for Balanchine's School of American Ballet and for the school of the San Francisco Ballet. The previous year, Michele had attended SAB, and I remember devouring her letters and imagining what it would be like to ride the bus or walk with her to class. Now, if the audition went well, it would be my turn.

Hundreds of girls from all over the state gathered at a local ballet school. For the San Francisco audition we were crammed into a studio with a number pinned to our leotard just above our chest. As two judges looked on, a teacher put us through the usual steps, starting with pliés at the barre and moving on to balancing, jumping and turning in the center of the room. After each group of combinations, the judges called out the numbers of the girls they were eliminating. Those who made it to the end had a good chance of receiving an acceptance letter. Michele and I were both still standing at the end.

The audition for SAB was entirely different. We were separated into age groups with twenty girls in each group and again given numbers to pin to our chests. Sheila had instructed us to wear white leotards and dance skirts to give us a clean, professional look. I had pinned little pink flowers in my hair. After waiting literally hours, my group was called into the studio.

The person in charge of the audition was Susan Hendl, a soloist with the New York City Ballet who would in time become one of the dearest and most supportive people in my life. Now she asked each of us to point first our right and then our left foot to the side as she assessed the curve of our arches. In ballet, a properly curved arch determines not only how your feet will move but also how they will look in pointe shoes. It was the lack of that arch that had prevented Sheila from becoming a ballerina, and I was now nervous that the right foot I'd injured in my riding accident would prevent me from being chosen.

The next thing Susie asked us to do was to lift one leg in the air, first to the front, then to the side, then to the back. At the height of the extension she took the leg in her hand and slowly stretched it to the ceiling to see how high it could potentially go. Mine went high.

In the end, both Michele and I were given full scholarships to the San Francisco Ballet School's intensive summer program. Since, much as I loved to dance, I had no sense that there was anything special about me, I wasn't really surprised or upset that I hadn't been offered a place at SAB.

For six weeks that summer, Michele and I really did ride the bus together. We also shared a room, and we took classes three times a day with girls from all over the country. At thirteen, I felt independent and grown-up.

In class, it was obvious that the teachers noticed me, but I had no idea whether I was getting their attention because I was good or because they noticed how hard I was working. It still didn't occur to me that I might be particularly talented.

When we returned to Sheila's class that fall, she was thrilled to announce that the New York City Ballet was going to be performing in Los Angeles, and Peter Martins, the gorgeous, Danish-born star of Balanchine's company, had agreed to teach one of our classes while they were in town. Of course, we all knew who Peter was, not only because he was such a big star but also because he was the lover of Heather Watts, a principal dancer with NYCB, who was one of Sheila's former students and perhaps her greatest success story.

On the appointed day we all dressed in our best leotards and anxiously awaited his arrival. When he didn't show up at the appointed time, Sheila started class without him. I had a sinking feeling that he wasn't going to come at all, but then the room suddenly grew silent and I turned to see a Greek god in white shorts standing in the doorway. I was stunned by Peter's physical presence, but even more stunned that he was going to be teaching my class.

To my amazement, he singled me out at the barre and encouraged me to turn my leg out even farther. He took a dime from his pocket and placed it on my heel while my leg was extended in front of me. If the dime didn't fall off, he said, I could keep it. I focused with all my might, and he actually laughed at how determined I was to keep that dime, but it stayed where he put it. For the first time I had a sense that there was an exciting world of ballet beyond Sheila's studio that I wanted to be part of. Needless to say, I hung on to that dime and stashed it away in my jewelry box for safekeeping.

By this time my younger sister, Romy, was also studying with Michele and me, and even though she was only eleven, the next year Sheila decided that all three of us could audition for the summer programs. We were thrilled when we all received scholarships to the San Francisco program, and I also got a full scholarship to the School of American Ballet.

As sisters, we decided that we'd all go to San Francisco together, but Sheila had other ideas. She called my mother and me into a conference and said that she thought it was time Michele and I were separated. I should go to New York while my sisters went to San Francisco. It seemed strange and a bit daunting to be going off without them, but my mother and I trusted Sheila, and ultimately I decided this was too much of an opportunity for me to pass up.

SEVEN

Oddly enough, even at fourteen, and in spite of all the warnings I'd heard about how dangerous it could be, I wasn't intimidated by being in New York. Just the opposite; I fell in love with the city. I was living with a woman who had rented me a room in her apartment on Central Park West just three blocks from Lincoln Center, and five other girls who had studied with Sheila and were also attending the summer program lived nearby, so I never really felt alone.

Monday through Friday we took two or three dance classes a day, but we had weekends off, and we were determined to experience as much of the city as we could cram into five short weeks. We saw the original Broadway production of *A Chorus Line* and went to Radio City Music Hall to see the Rockettes. We walked up and down Fifth Avenue and splurged on brunch at Windows on the World at the top of the World Trade Center.

What did intimidate me, however, was the School of American Ballet. In San Francisco, the teachers had all known my name and always made sure that I had a place in the center of the studio. At SAB it was entirely different. Once we finished at the barre and moved to the floor, everyone had to scramble for a good position, and the most confident girls always made sure they were front and center where the teacher would notice them. The classes were huge, and if you didn't get a prime spot, there was no way you'd be seen. I knew that, but I just didn't have the confidence or the nerve to push my way to the front.

In addition, as I looked around me, I could see how much better than I the other girls were. While I could barely turn twice and didn't jump very high (at least in my own mind), they all seemed to turn like tops and leap like birds soaring across the sky. These were the girls who had always dreamed of being ballerinas. They had smooth, straight hair held in perfect buns and stage mothers waiting for them outside the classroom. In that milieu I knew I wasn't going to stand out, but I was happy for my New York experience—and even happier to be going back to Sheila's at the end of the summer.

Sheila's studio, however, was just about the only place I was happy. My situation at home and at school was not going well.

About three years earlier my mother's boyfriend, Dave, had moved in with us. He shod horses at Rhonda and Michael's ranch, and they'd thought he and my mom would get along, so they introduced them. At first we were all happy to have him around. A big, six-foot-five, burly guy, Dave not only loved to go riding with us, he was also my mom's folk-dancing partner and a perennial fixer-upper. He came over to fix things around our house and was always available to drive me to Hebrew school or ballet class. By the time he moved in, it seemed as if he were already part of the family. But that's not exactly what Dave had in mind.

One evening after he'd been living with us for a few months, he sat all four of us kids down and, with his arm around my mother, announced that they were moving to Alaska and we would be going to live with our dad. We all sat there quietly waiting for Mom to say something, but she didn't.

Afterward, Michele and I went outside to meet our friends as we did every evening, only this time we told them that we'd be moving. I knew my mother had been totally devoted to us for years, and I wanted her to be happy. But I also wanted her to stay.

In the end, they didn't go. (Later she told me that she'd never have gone through with the plan, but she never did say why she'd allowed him to make the announcement in the first place). Dave was stuck with us and he resented that. He let his anger show to the point where it was dangerous to provoke him in any way. Michele was already sixteen and able to simply ignore him. Gary and Romy were basically nonconfrontational kids, but when Dave started to boss me around, I lashed out, reminding him in no uncertain terms that he wasn't my father and had no right to tell me what to do.

The more I resisted him, the more we fought. In addition to being verbally abusive, he'd hold me under the cold water in the shower when he thought I was being too temperamental, and once when we went riding he whipped me with the reins. What made his behavior even more confusing was that he could also be incredibly supportive. He drove me to ballet class, beamed at my performances in Sheila's year-end recitals, and had been the only one in my family present when I got a reward for receiving straight A's on my report card. The stress of coping with his Jekyll and Hyde personality was getting to me, and I was also starting to fight with my neighborhood friends, many of whom had problems of their own. The only place I had to feel good about myself when I wasn't with Gent was at Sheila's studio, and I started to spend more and more time there.

By now I was in Sheila's most advanced class, which didn't begin until seven in the evening, but Sheila allowed all students to take as many lower-level classes as they wanted free of charge. Since I was fighting with my friends, I couldn't hang out with them, so I did my homework in the library during my lunch hour, and because I didn't want to go home after school, I took the bus directly to Sheila's. Some days I took as many as four classes in a row, including my sister Romy's.

By this time, Michele was less interested in ballet and more in cheerleading, but Romy was becoming more interested and more serious about her dancing.

At night the two of us practiced in the kitchen, using the counter as our barre and trying to lift our legs as high as we could without hitting Mom in the head while she cooked.

My ongoing battles with Dave came to a head early one Sunday morning. I was supposed to go to Sunday school, but that was the only morning of the week when I could sleep late, and I just didn't want to get out of bed. My mother kept yelling at me to get up, until she finally came back into the room one more time and screamed, "I'm not going to tell you one more time. Get up!"

Still, I pretended to be asleep. Then, suddenly, I heard a huge roar, like that of a wild animal. The next thing I knew Dave's enormous body was on top of mine. His hands were around my throat, heaving me up and down as I gasped for air. I went limp, certain that I had just taken my last breath when I heard my mother screaming, "Get off her. Get off!" Finally, somehow, she pulled him away as I lay there shaking.

Half an hour later, my mom was driving us all to Sunday school. We were silent in the car, and it would be many years before we ever talked about what had happened. The next day Dave drove me to ballet class. He acted as if nothing was wrong, but he must have known that he'd finally gone too far.

Up to that point, even though he'd been abusive, I wasn't afraid of Dave—at least not afraid enough to keep quiet when I was angry. That Sunday, however, with his hands around my throat in a blind rage, I was shocked into the sudden realization that he really could have hurt me. Without ever coming to a conscious decision, I stopped speaking up after that. I also prayed that my mother would ask Dave to leave our house. A few weeks later, while my sisters, my brother and I were on a camping trip with our dad and his new wife, Lynn, I got my wish. When we came back on Sunday night, the house was quiet and Dave was gone.

* * *

That year, I was again awarded a scholarship to the SAB summer program, and all three of us—Michele, Romy and I—also won scholarships to San Francisco. For me, SAB was the major leagues, but I still wasn't convinced I was good enough to be there and I didn't really think my teachers liked me. So again, I decided to go to San Francisco with my sisters. And again, Sheila would have none of it. This time, when she called my mother and me into her office, she announced that I *had* to go to SAB. "I've never seen a dancer as talented as Zippora," she said. "I know she belongs in New York. I've never felt so sure about anything."

I was stunned. I knew Sheila thought I was good, but I had no idea she thought I was so special.

EIGHT

Over the past year I had grown four inches, and all the dancing I was doing had made my legs stronger. I was able to complete more turns and my jumps were higher. At SAB that summer it was clear the combination of my physical growth and the work I'd put in had catapulted me to a new level. Although I still struggled with certain steps, I no longer thought of myself as inferior to the other students. I could feel the changes in my body, and I was dancing with a newfound confidence.

And for the first time the faculty was noticing me; my instructors now knew me by name.

At the end of the summer session, all the students lined up for a meeting with Madame Gleboff, the associate director of SAB and one of the many Russians on the faculty, to receive an evaluation of our work. When it was my turn, I entered her office and nervously offered my name. Madame Gleboff, an administrator who had never been a dancer, was a woman in her fifties with brownish hair and a businesslike manner. Without even glancing up from the list in front of her, she said, "Zippora, you are an excellent dancer. We have had a hard time coming to a conclusion about you because we don't know how you feel about staying for the fall. We didn't dare ask your mother, either. But if you don't stay next year it will be too late. If you don't stay between fourteen and sixteen years old, it's unprofessional."

I could hardly believe what I was hearing. I was being offered a place in Balanchine's school! Too shocked and intimidated to say what I really thought, which was "I'm flattered, but you are crazy! I'm only fifteen years old," I muttered something about my parents' wanting me to go to college, thanked her and left the office, walking past the line of girls still waiting, each of them hoping and praying to be told what I'd just been told.

I still wasn't thinking about dancing professionally, and, in any case, I knew that we didn't have the money for my tuition, room and board, so I decided I wouldn't even mention Madam Gleboff's invitation to my mother.

I got home the last week in July, in time for the final week of classes before Sheila's studio closed for a month-long summer break. That first day back, I wanted her and my fellow students to see how much I'd improved over the summer, and I showed off a bit, holding my balances as long as I could and lifting my legs as high as possible.

At the end of class, I hung back as each girl did her "reverence," bowing to the teacher and shaking her hand. When all the others had left, it was my turn. I couldn't wait to give Sheila my news because I knew how proud she would be.

"How did it go this summer?" she asked.

"They liked me much better this year," I replied. "They even asked me to stay on for the winter."

Without a word, Sheila grabbed me by the hand. As she pulled me out the door to where my mother was waiting to drive me home, she uttered one two-word exclamation: "You're going!"

PART THREE

Dancing for Balanchine

NINE

Once Sheila made her announcement, everything happened so fast that I didn't have much time to think about it. The first thing we had to find out was whether I could receive any financial assistance, because Sheila's enthusiasm wasn't going to pay the bills. I knew it was difficult for my mother to make the call to SAB; she didn't like asking for help. But the school's administrator called her back the same day to say that I'd not only been awarded a full scholarship, but that it came with some amazing "extras." The scholarship, funded by the Atlantic Richfield Company, was given to just one student each year, and in addition to SAB's tuition it also covered tuition for my academic studies at the Professional Children's School, a private school for working child actors, dancers and singers, as well as free lunches in the school cafeteria, $300 per month for living expenses, and two round-trip tickets home during the year.

Even though I'd been on my own in New York for the past two summers, this was different, and I knew it. While Dave was living with us, all I dreamed of was getting out of the house, but now that he was gone I wasn't sure that's what I really wanted. I even caught myself secretly hoping that something would happen to keep me from going. But nothing did, and I never mentioned my trepidations to my mom. I think she understood that I was having mixed feelings, but, to her credit, she never pressured me either to go or to stay. As it turned out, Deidre, a friend from the summer program who lived in Florida, had also been invited to become a full-time student, so at least I'd have one friend.

When the time finally arrived, saying goodbye to my family was even harder than I had imagined it would be. My dad cried as we took our final run on the beach together at the end of our annual summer camping trip. The only other time I'd seen him shed a tear was when his father died. On that last morning, he told me he was crying because he'd never gotten to spend as much time with me as he would have wanted, and now I was leaving.

Romy, with whom I'd become so close, felt totally abandoned and wouldn't even speak to me at times. Even though she was happy for me, the only way she could express her emotions was by shutting me out.

And then there was Gent, who had been not only my best friend but my responsibility. Even though I knew I couldn't pass up the opportunity I'd been given, I felt terribly guilty about leaving him.

Strangely, however, saying goodbye to Dave was the saddest of all. He still came around from time to time to finish up some yard work he'd never completed, and one afternoon, when my mother and I got home from a shopping expedition to buy me a winter coat, he was out there. As Mom went inside, he called me over and handed me a package containing a big, coffee-table-type book. I don't remember the title, but I do still remember the inscription. It read, "Guys like me only dream of doing in life what you're doing. I'm so proud of you. Love, Dave."

As it turned out, that was the last time I ever saw him. He died of cancer a few years later, and even though he'd caused me so much pain, it saddened me to think of him dying so young, troubled and alone.

TEN

On the plane, I sat in a window seat staring out at the clouds. For the first time in weeks, I had a chance to really reflect on how my life was going to change, and what that would mean. I couldn't help thinking of Julie Andrews in *The Sound of Music*, my favorite movie when I was a little girl. I remembered the scene in which Maria is sent out of the convent to start a new life she knows nothing about. To keep up her courage, she sings "I have confidence in me." As the plane approached New York, I sang the line to myself. I felt corny even then, but, like Maria, I, too, was embarking on a new life, and beneath the brave face I was showing the world, I was also terrified. Things had turned out pretty well for Maria in the movie, and I was hoping they would for me, too.

I soon discovered that there was little about SAB's summer program to prepare me for this new experience. In the summer, groups of little girls with flowers in their chignons and dreams of sugar plums in their heads had lined the hallways, stretching their legs while they talked and whispered between classes. All the summer students were new to the school, and we'd wander the hallways not knowing which studio we were supposed to be in.

Now I felt like I was the only new kid. Everyone but me seemed to know exactly where they were supposed to be. They knew all the teachers and they knew one another. They were busy greeting one another and catching up after the summer vacation while I stood there feeling totally lost. They were serious and they looked serious, too. Unlike the summer students, who had dressed in brightly colored leotards hoping to attract attention, the winter students were required to wear the basic ballet uniform of black leotards for morning class and white for afternoon pointe class.

Leg warmers and sweatshirts were allowed only during the first thirty minutes or so when we were at the barre. Another important rule at SAB in the winter was that all students wear pointe shoes for every class, even at the barre and even when we weren't dancing on pointe, because Balanchine wanted our toes so developed that we would have as much control over them as we had over our fingers. Wearing pointe shoes every day, morning and afternoon, helped us achieve that strength because the shoe itself offered a degree of resistance you don't feel when you're wearing practice slippers.

At Sheila's and in San Francisco, we wore pointe shoes only every other day and never at the barre. Beyond that, New York was a lot colder than California, even in the fall, and my toes were always freezing. Even as a child I had a circulation problem, and my toes were colder than anyone else's. Now I had to get to class as early as possible to warm up my toes before putting on my pointe shoes. Even with warm toes, however, dancing on pointe at every single class took an immediate toll on my calves and I developed shin splints, which was a common injury for first-time winter students at SAB. So, in addition to warming my toes before class, I was icing my shins afterward.

All this newness was intimidating, and I really missed home. My mother and Romy were calling me every night. While all the people around me seemed so certain of what they wanted—to dance with City Ballet—I didn't yet know whether or not that was what I wanted for myself.

The biggest change besides dancing during the day and into early evening was having my academic studies scheduled around dance. I'd wake up in the morning and go to my first period class at the Professional Children's School, where the majority of high school students were SAB dancers. After first period we would get together and walk the six blocks to the ballet studio in the Juilliard building. There, we'd change into our practice clothes, warm up our bodies and take our first class, which ran from ten-thirty to twelve. Then we'd change back into street clothes and disperse for lunch. After lunch, I'd go to fifth- and sixth-period classes at PCS, then back to SAB for a second ballet class, and on some evenings we would take our third ballet class of the day.

I was expected to do the remainder of my academic work on my own, meeting with the teacher just once a week to go over assignments. That was also new for me, and I found that I missed the direction and the opportunity to ask questions that I'd been used to in regular classes. Altogether, it was a big adjustment.

After the first two weeks, I was told that Madame Gleboff wanted to see me. Walking down the hall, I was sure she was going to say that giving me such a generous scholarship had been a big mistake. I didn't think I was any worse than the other girls in my class, but I also didn't think I was outstanding, so it seemed reasonable to me that SAB would have reached the same conclusion. When I got to her office, however, she told me that Deidre and I would be moving up to the next level.

Deidre was a long-legged redhead who danced like a gazelle and, for her age, was one of the most sensual dancers I'd ever seen. We were the only two in our class to be moved up, and we would now be in the second-highest level, which was one of the main classes from which Balanchine chose new dancers for his company. I was just getting used to my original class and was beginning to make friends. I wasn't ready to be thrust into a class where most of the other girls were sixteen to eighteen, looked their age and were ready to become professional dancers. I was fifteen, but I looked two or three years younger. When I walked into my new class for the first time, I could feel the cold stares of the older girls, who were clearly wondering who I was and what I was doing there. Truthfully, I couldn't blame them, because I didn't really know what I was doing there, either.

I found a place at the barre and set down my dance bag, which was filled with the usual dancer's paraphernalia: practice slippers, leg warmers and pointe shoes. As I started to warm up, stretching my legs and sliding into a split, one of the older girls loomed above me and announced, "That's my place." The way she said it made me feel that I should just pick up my bag and leave, but I quickly apologized and found another spot. Still, my legs shook so much during the entire class that I could hardly hold a balance. I wanted to justify why I was there by dancing well, but I was an anxious mess.

Another terrifying experience was my first partnering class, in which we were taught how to perform a pas de deux, a dance for two people, usually a man and a woman. The class was taught by the Russian-born Andrei Kramarevsky, who spoke little English and gave us very difficult combinations to perform, as all the Russian teachers would. When someone did something well, he would say, "Expensive!" meaning the dancing was good and worth a lot of money.

It was frightening for several reasons. First of all, I was afraid no one would want to partner me. The girls who were easiest to partner—the ones the advanced boys liked to dance with—turned easily and jumped effortlessly. That wasn't me. Besides that, except for playing Truth or Dare in sixth grade a few times, I'd never really been touched by a boy before. And, to make matters worse, the boys were the best male dancers at SAB, and intimidating because they were so cool. When I walked into the studio that first day, some of the guys broke into laughter. One of them had probably just told a joke, but I was convinced they were laughing at me.

What had I gotten myself into? A month ago I was about to enter my junior year of high school, and the most important decision I thought I'd have to make was where I wanted to attend college in two years. Now I was surrounded by incredibly ambitious, competitive and talented people who seemed like they would stop at nothing to get what every one of them wanted— a career as a professional dancer. I loved dancing, and by now I was getting the sense that I was good at it, but at that point I didn't have that drive or ambition, and I still wasn't sure that this was the career I wanted for myself.

After the first day in my new class, I talked to Romy, as I did every night, and cried as I told her what a hard time I was having and that I just wanted to use one of the free tickets I'd been given and book a flight home. Although she was only twelve years old, I chose to talk to her about what was going on instead of burdening my mother with my problems. I didn't want my mom to worry about me, and if I told her how unhappy I was, there was no way she wouldn't worry. I felt like a fish out of water and didn't know if I wanted to put myself through this.

Thankfully, I didn't go home, because, within weeks, everything changed for me. The level I'd been placed in gave me the opportunity to study with the greatest teachers in the world. My main teachers were Suki Schorer, Alexandra Danilova, Antonina

Tumkovsky, Muriel Stuart, Helene Dudin and Stanley Williams, who had been Peter Martins's boyhood teacher and Sheila's favorite when she observed classes at SAB. Each one of them had been personally chosen by George Balanchine, and each of them was unique. They had different backgrounds, different training and different styles, but they were all at the highest level of their art form, each working in his or her own way to help us achieve Balanchine's vision. As I watched them and learned from them, it was as if the entire history of dance had come alive for me in the classroom.

One of my favorite teachers was the former NYCB principal dancer Suki Schorer, a petite fireball of energy with short blond hair who always came to class in a basic leotard with a colored skirt. Balanchine had recognized her talent for teaching when she was still a dancer in his company, and had asked her take new company members aside and instruct them privately. Then, when she retired, she became a full-time teacher at SAB. Suki had a lot of inspirational words of wisdom, one of which was the line Balanchine frequently used with his dancers: "What are you waiting for? The time to rest is in the grave!" Another, which she used to motivate us when we were holding an arabesque, with one leg high in the air behind us and the opposite arm reaching to the front, was: "What do you like, diamonds? Ice cream? Reach for it!"

Because I was still having trouble doing multiple turns and high jumps, I loved the fact that she focused on transitions—getting into the jump or landing from it—rather than just on how many turns we could do or how high we leaped. Suki helped me to stop obsessing about my weak turns and jumps and start giving equal attention to the dance as a whole.

The ultimate teacher for the Zen of dancing, however, was Stanley Williams. In his mid-fifties, slender, with thinning gray hair, Stanley taught class like a pipe-smoking Buddhist monk meditating. He always directed the pianist to play just a few notes, slowly and quietly, like a soft drumbeat, even when we moved fast. He didn't say much, but what he did say was profound.

One of his brief pronouncements that really affected me was "technique is timing." I took this to mean that instead of attempting to dance steps, as I had been doing, by using brute strength, it was more effective, though in some ways more difficult, to let the music be the force that carried me. Stanley's approach to teaching was very different from Suki's, but it was sublime and it worked. I was turning and jumping better than I ever had.

Stanley was also known throughout the world as the paramount teacher of male dancers. In addition to Peter Martins, the great Erik Bruhn had studied with him, and Rudolf Nureyev credited Stanley's classes with lengthening his compact muscles and called him "a true genius." I remember watching Nureyev in Stanley's class, working at the barre between Mikhail Baryshnikov and Peter Martins. As a fifteen-year-old, I knew I was witnessing something great, but looking back today I recognize the extraordinary moment I was present for—watching as potentially the three greatest male dancers of all time took a class together.

Like groupies at a rock concert, the girls at SAB crowded

around the two doors of the studio to watch all the gorgeous men in black tights taking the advanced class. Baryshnikov and Peter Martins would be joking with each other one minute and trying to outdo each other with multiple turns the next. I was especially thrilled that when Peter was in class he'd sometimes give me a wink to let me know he remembered me.

But it wasn't just the men who were gorgeous. All the City Ballet dancers looked to me like the most beautiful people in the world. When they walked they glided, and when they danced their bodies sang. I didn't really believe that I would ever be as beautiful as they were, but I knew that I could learn to move as they moved and to express myself with my body as eloquently as they did. Seeing them, and knowing that I was actually a part of this magical, creative kingdom had a profound impact on me. It seemed that, almost in an instant, I was literally swept up in a world I had never known existed, and I suddenly felt as if I were being reborn. No longer did I doubt that I belonged here. Sheila's vision for me had been to dance for Balanchine, and now that was my vision, too. This had become the only place I wanted to be.

Before class, I still sometimes felt like the little sister who had somehow crashed the big kids' party, but once the teacher entered the room and the music began, we all wanted the same thing. We knew that each teacher had some wisdom to impart that would help us develop into the dancers we longed to be. Every student in that room wanted to be a great dancer, and, specifically, to dance with the New York City Ballet.

* * *

The creator of this entire magical kingdom was George Balanchine, or Mr. B, as he was called. When I first arrived at SAB, I thought that Mr. B was the six-four, grim-faced man I saw every day in the hallways, the one with the slow, deliberate gait who always wore a black suit and a frown. But that was actually Lincoln Kirstein, a daunting and distant authority figure who had been responsible for bringing Balanchine to America. The real Balanchine, as it turned out, was nothing like that. Nor was he what I imagined a genius would be. In fact, there was something extremely approachable about him, and he wasn't at all intimidating. The first time I passed him in the hallway, I wasn't sure if I should look away or look down. As he walked by, I ended up looking right at him, and he looked directly into my eyes and smiled. I was immediately struck by how nonthreatening he seemed.

When I started my first year as a full-time student at SAB, Balanchine was seventy-six years old. He was of medium height, slim and very serene. Pictures of him as a young man show him to have been extremely handsome, with fine features that gave him the look of a painter or a poet. Now his still-handsome face reflected his dignity and wisdom.

His usual attire, consisting of a Western shirt and string tie, reflected the love that this man who had been born Georgi Melitonovitch Balanchivadze in Russia had for the American West.

From what I've read of Balanchine's early days at the Imperial Theater School in St. Petersburg, which he entered at the age of nine, his initial impressions of ballet were very much like my own.

He couldn't figure out why he was being asked to put his body in such awkward positions; he was convinced he couldn't do it, and, even if he could do it, he didn't much want to.

Then, in his second year, he was chosen to perform the "Garland Dance" in a production of *The Sleeping Beauty*. Overwhelmed by the beautifully painted sets, the gorgeous costumes, and the way the dancers moved to the sublime Tchaikovsky music, he fell in love with ballet. He was ten years old.

Balanchine was just eighteen when he established his own small company of fifteen dancers, including his then sixteen-year-old bride, Tamara Geva, and his future common-law wife, Alexandra Danilova, who would become a great ballerina in her own right and who was still teaching at SAB when I arrived. In fact, during my first year as a full-time student, I was honored to be chosen to dance a solo in *Reflections of a Dancer,* a documentary film about Danilova's life. To dance in the film as she coached me was a privilege beyond imagining.

Although Balanchine revered the great, full-length classical ballets he had been brought up on (*Don Quixote, La Bayadère, The Sleeping Beauty, The Nutcracker* and *Swan Lake,* created by Marius Petipa for the Russian ballet in the late-ninteenth and early-twentieth centuries), the ballets he choreographed, from the very beginning, had no princes, no swan queens, no lavish sets. Rather, they featured a man, a woman, the dancers surrounding them and the music, which supplied the impetus for every move they made.

On July 4, 1924, Balanchine left Russia with a troupe of four dancers including Geva and Danilova, to perform in Germany. From there they went on to England, where Balanchine received a telegram from Serge Diaghilev, the legendary founder and director of the Ballets Russes, inviting him and his company to audition. Within days, they had become part of the Ballets Russes, and Balanchine's life was changed forever. Years later, he would tell his biographer, Bernard Taper, "It is because of Diaghilev that I am whatever I am today."

Five years later, however, on August 19, 1929, Diaghilev died suddenly in Venice, and Balanchine was once more on his own. In what must surely be one of the most serendipitous occurrences of all time, Lincoln Kirstein, a wealthy young American with good connections and great determination, was vacationing in Venice and happened to wander into the church where Diaghilev's funeral was being conducted. A lover of the arts, especially ballet, Kirstein was already familiar with Balanchine's ballets. Now, taking this unlikely occurrence as a sign, he decided that he was meant to bring ballet home to America and popularize it.

He and Balanchine did not actually meet, however, until 1933. In the meantime, Balanchine was freelancing as much as he could and, in the process, becoming increasingly bored and annoyed with European ballet, which he regarded as stale and creatively stifling.

At that first meeting, arranged by a mutual friend, Kirstein asked Balanchine, "What do you want to do?"

"I want to come to America," Balanchine said, adding that he would love to go to a place where there were girls as wonderful as Ginger Rogers.

"I'll get you to America," Kirstein promised.

But Balanchine knew that getting to America was just the beginning. Yes, he would have the artistic freedom he craved and needed, but dancers would be in short supply because, at that time, American dancers were poorly trained.

So, when Kirstein promised him not only his own company but also his own theater, Balanchine insisted on setting the priorities.

"But first, a school," he said.

The School of American Ballet opened its doors in 1934, a year after Kirstein and Balanchine's first meeting. Fourteen years after that, New York City Ballet gave its first performance.

ELEVEN

The 1980–81 City Ballet season began in November, following six weeks of rehearsal, and I finally had my first opportunity to see a Balanchine ballet performed onstage. Deidre and I were determined to see as many performances as we possibly could. Sometimes we bought standing-room tickets, but we couldn't afford to buy tickets every night, so we came up with a scheme. We would wait until we saw company members entering through the backstage door. Then we'd tag along, hoping that the guard would assume we were among the new dancers Balanchine had picked from our class. Once inside, we'd make our way backstage and out a secret door to the front of the house, where we had to sneak past the usher. The one who looked like a blond witch always knew what we were up to and watched us like a hawk. We hid in the bathroom until the lights went down, and when she was busy seating last-minute arrivals we'd sneak into the theater and find empty seats.

One night the ballerina dancing Titania, one of the leading

roles in Balanchine's *A Midsummer's Night Dream,* was so breath-taking that I was sure she must be the great Suzanne Farrell, whom I had heard so much about but had not yet seen in person. But when I looked in my program, I saw that Titania was being danced by Nina Federova. I tried to find her name among the listed company dancers but didn't see it anywhere.

In ballet companies, dancers are assigned to one of three ranks: the highest ranked are principal dancers, followed by soloists. Principals and soloists dance leading roles. Most dancers in any company, however, are in the third rank, the corps de ballet, which literally means "body of the ballet." Corps dancers are the ones whose names you don't know. They're the dancers who perform in nearly every ballet, often positioned onstage behind the principals and doing the same steps the principals do.

It hadn't occurred to me to look for Federova's name among the corps de ballet dancers. At the time I wasn't aware that Balanchine was known for giving dancers in the corps a chance to perform major roles. But Federova was indeed a corps dancer. I couldn't believe it. Knowing that this was how good dancers in the corps were, I felt especially intimidated.

After a while, Deidre figured out that we didn't have to buy tickets or sneak past the usher to see a performance. Instead, we'd enter the theater through the stage door and take the elevator up to the level where the stagehands, operating from a catwalk, pulled the scenery up and down. There was a tiny bench at the front of the catwalk where they allowed us to sit and peer down at the stage so long as we didn't get in their way.

We had to lean from side to side as the scenery went up and down, but I liked being up there because we also got to see what was going on backstage. The dancers would smile as they danced for the audience, but the moment they were offstage the smile was gone and they were leaning over, hands on knees, gasping for breath. Then they would joke or talk or yawn. They'd adjust their costumes and their shoes. They'd sit and massage their aches and pains. They'd run in place to keep their muscles warm. I'd put them all on such a pedestal that seeing them this way made them a bit more human to me.

From my perch high above the stage, I picked out my favorites in the corps, but no one I watched came even close to having the effect on me that Suzanne Farrell did when I finally did get to see her dance. The more I watched her, the more I fell in love with the way she danced. She wasn't a perfect technician. Some nights she would fall off her balances, some nights she hit balances that seemed to last for days. But she was the most spontaneous, thrilling performer I'd ever seen or possibly will ever see again. Some people dance *to* the music; Suzanne *was* the music. Watching her, I understood Balanchine's maxim, "See the music, hear the dance." She was everything I wanted to be.

I was also intrigued by her relationship with Balanchine. She had joined City Ballet when she was sixteen years old, and although Balanchine was forty-one years older than she, and married, he fell madly in love with her. The situation was complicated; nevertheless, Suzanne became his muse.

Despite Balanchine's love and attention, Suzanne eventually married a fellow company member, Paul Mejia. Prior to their marriage, Mejia had been given some good roles; after it, Balanchine did not cast him.

Consequently, they both left NYCB to dance in the company of the brilliant modernist Maurice Béjart. Suzanne danced beautifully in Béjart's company, but her soul belonged to Mr. B. Her home and her heart were always with Balanchine and she came back to the company. Watching her dance, I felt that I was witnessing a historic event, the master and his muse reunited.

The more I watched not only Suzanne but all the dancers in the company perform, the more in awe I became of what I was seeing.

That first year, Suzanne taught my Monday morning class. There she stood, ten feet away, my idol, with a perfect Balanchine body—long, slender legs, nice arches, long neck, small head—no makeup, hair in a ponytail, wearing a simple leotard, practice skirt and pointe shoes.

Whenever she taught, she brought with her handfuls of pointe shoes that had been made specifically for her feet but that, for one reason or another, she had chosen to discard. I always took a pair because even though they were a bit too small, I could fit my feet into her shoes and I was determined to wear them.

Balanchine used to say that he could tell how a dancer danced by the way she did her *tendu*. A *tendu* is accomplished by standing on one leg with the other leg extended straight out to the front, side or back. The foot is arched; the toes are fully pointed. The second, third and big toe gently touch the floor. Suzanne had the perfect *tendu.* I had never seen it done so beautifully and perfectly. I had never thought a *tendu* could be so important or that I would be so obsessed by such a simple movement. Now I wanted to do it as perfectly as she did.

Suzanne pushed me further than I thought I could be pushed. She'd have us do a step that we counted in four counts while the music played in three counts. She'd give us a combination and then say "Reverse" while we were in the middle of it. She'd have us hold a balance for the count of eight, an impossible feat. But even if we couldn't do it, she wanted us to try. I often felt clumsy in her classes, but I never felt inadequate. She gave me exactly what I needed: the freedom to explore without fear of failure.

She took the shame out of not being perfect.

TWELVE

Mr. B spent most of his time at the theater, four blocks from SAB, but he came by the school occasionally, mostly when he was looking for new dancers. He would appear unexpectedly, and we all knew that at any moment he could walk into a class, look at you, like you, pick you for the company and, in that moment, transform your life—even if you weren't one of the dancers favored by the administration and teachers at SAB.

We all knew the stories about dancers like Heather Watts, Sheila's former pupil. When Sheila had joyously told us about Heather's promotion to principal dancer, what she hadn't mentioned was that Heather was as difficult and disruptive as she was talented. But that feistiness didn't deter Mr. B. He took her into the company because he knew that she was supremely talented and that he would be able to bring out the best in her.

I was in Suki's class one morning when Balanchine made one of his surprise visits. We were doing a series of high leg lifts that were to be executed slowly—a movement called an *adagio*. I looked to the front of the room, and there he stood. For a second, time seemed to stand still; you could have heard a pin drop. Then, in the blink of an eye, sweatshirts were pulled off, tights and leotards were pulled perfectly into place.

One girl in the class was extraordinarily beautiful and a very nice dancer, but she was a party girl and absent much of the time. There were constant rumors that SAB was going to suspend her, maybe even expel her, but as luck would have it, she was in class that day, and Balanchine could not take his eyes off her. Soon we heard that she had been made a member of his company, where she would go on to dance for many years.

Events like that gave life at SAB an air of unlimited possibility.

Besides being seen in the right class at the right time, the best chance a student had of being noticed was in the year-end workshop performances. The audience for these performances included every major dance critic in New York City, many of New York City Ballet's principal dancers, and the most important choreographers and company directors of the time—Balanchine, Robbins, Baryshnikov, Nureyev and Twyla Tharp, among others. If you had a good role in a workshop and danced it well, the odds were pretty good that you'd get a job with some company.

Each year the program was comprised of approximately six pieces, generally great works restaged by SAB teachers that called upon dancers to perform in different styles. And the class I'd been moved up to was one of the two from which students were chosen for parts in the program.

The City Ballet teachers and dancers who were presenting pieces all came to watch our classes and choose the dancers for their casts. The first year I was there, I danced in four of the six ballets. Now I was not only watching Balanchine's ballets; I was actually learning and dancing them myself. I was becoming fully a part of Mr. B's magical kingdom. That year I was in the corps of Balanchine's *La Source,* staged by Suki. Deidre and I danced a pas de trois originally choreographed by August Bournonville for the Royal Danish Ballet and staged that year by the New York City Ballet principal dancer, Adam Luders. The third ballet I danced in was a new work by NYCB soloist Joseph Duell, and the fourth was *The Magic Flute,* newly choreographed by Peter Martins.

This was the first year that Balanchine asked Peter to choreograph for the workshop, and I was elated to be cast as a demi soloist, and even more excited when, soon after rehearsals began, Peter asked me to also understudy the leading role (as a demi soloist I was one of four dancers highlighted from the corp de ballet). I was scared and didn't think I was ready for a lead at that point, it was incredibly exciting to be chosen and to be dancing a part Peter Martins had choreographed for me. I loved the fact that Peter liked me, and I was thrilled by the promise of more leads in my future.

Balanchine came to all of the final workshop rehearsals. It was the first time I'd ever danced for him, and I'm sure that all the other dancers hoped, as I did, that he would notice us. He really did give us all the sense that he noticed everyone and everything. Peeking at him out of the corner of my eye, trying not to stare,

I was wondering what he was saying. Who was he watching? What did he think? I didn't want to miss a single gesture.

But even when Balanchine wasn't at rehearsal, there was always some godlike important person there watching: Peter Martins, Jerry Robbins, even Baryshnikov. And I was one of the people they were looking at.

There was enormous pressure to perform well, of course, because we'd been rehearsing our parts for the entire school year, but for me it was also an enormous amount of fun. I was still one of the "new kids," and the pressure wasn't as great as it was for some of the older, more experienced students. Also, one thing I knew about myself was that no matter how insecure I might feel offstage or in rehearsal, when the curtain went up I danced my heart out. I loved being onstage, and steps that I may have struggled over in the classroom always seemed to work when it came time for the actual performance.

I knew I'd done well in my workshop performances, but I didn't know whether any of my teachers would be considering me for a lead the following year. My secret fantasy was that I'd at least get to learn a lead as an understudy, but I didn't dare to hope for more than that.

I went home for the summer feeling really good about myself. In addition to discovering my passion at SAB, I'd made new friends who enjoyed being with me and who never thought of me as the "bad Zippora." Back in California, I took driving lessons and got my license. I rode Gent, spent time with my family, took classes with Sheila and dreamed of getting back to New York.

THIRTEEN

During my second year at SAB, I was becoming technically stronger and artistically more mature. In October, Suki cast me as the leading ballerina in the third movement of Balanchine's *Brahms-Schoenberg Quartet,* the ballet she'd be presenting in that year's workshop performance. The role was both romantic and grand, and I was naturally thrilled.

Balanchine had choreographed the role for Allegra Kent, one of his most divine, musical and mysterious ballerinas. She had retired the month before I arrived in New York in 1980, so I never actually saw her perform, but I'd watched her on videotape. I was thrilled to be dancing a role that had been created for her.

I also had a lead in the ballet Stanley staged that year, another piece by Bournonville, and again Deidre was in it with me. I was learning a lot of new ballets, and I found that memorizing the choreography wasn't hard. Dancers are able to perform an amazing variety of works and learn an unbelievable amount of choreography because of what is called kinetic memory, or muscle memory, which is what makes it possible to execute complex movements without conscious thought.

Every dancer is born with this ability to one degree or another, but all dancers will benefit from the guidance of an experienced teacher. Some teachers are more adept than others at conveying choreography. There are different ways a teacher learns the steps and counts of a ballet. Is he teaching a role that has been choreographed specifically for him, or is it a role he has just watched other dancers perform? Sometimes the teacher learns a dance from a videotape (which can be accompanied by notes), and has had no firsthand experience of the exact counts and timing.

When she was teaching, Suki often danced the steps herself so we could see exactly how to do them, but Stanley taught differently. As I've said, he was not a man of many words, and those he spoke were often uttered so quietly that they could be hard to understand.

The Bournonville piece opened with three men dancing a fast, complicated sequence. When the boys rehearsed it, their unison was totally off. They clearly did not know the counts. Day after day I watched them making the same mistakes. Stanley would glance over at Deidre and me with a look that said, *What am I to do with them?* Looking back, I can't believe I had the nerve to do this, but one day I actually asked Stanley if I could take over the rehearsal.

"If you think you can help, please do," he said, looking amused.

I then proceeded to tell the men what the counts were and

made them do the sequence over and over until they got it right. I could feel the "Boss" in me being reborn just as I could feel the stirrings of my future as a teacher.

When they finally got it, Stanley looked at me with a smile. "My," he said, taking a puff of his cigar, "you are one tough cookie!"

From then on, to my delight, Tough Cookie became his nickname for me.

In mid-December I flew home for the school holidays. On my first day back I was anxious to get behind the wheel and use the driver's license I'd acquired the previous summer. My mom agreed to let me drive her and Romy to see the horses, which were now in a pasture not far from where we lived. We were just a few miles from our house when a woman coming out of an intersection ran a red light at full speed and plowed into the driver's side of our car. What happened in an instant seemed like slow motion. Our car spun around, and when it finally stopped, I looked up and saw my mother and my sister covered in blood. As it turned out, Romy had broken her collarbone and my mother had only superficial cuts. I thought I was fine except for a little pain in my leg; I just felt terribly guilty because I was the one driving. But when I put my hand down to feel my leg, there was what felt like a giant hole where the car door had punctured the outside of my left thigh.

By then someone had helped us out of the car and someone must have called 911, because an ambulance arrived and I was taken on a stretcher to the hospital. The doctors stitched me up and said I was going to be fine; I was lucky because if the wound had been any deeper it would have cut into the muscle and I would never have walked again. All I could think about was that if Suki found out, she wouldn't let me dance the Brahms.

I recuperated at home for the two weeks of vacation and decided that I wouldn't tell anyone at SAB about the injury. I was able to walk without a limp or visible pain, and because I changed into my tights before getting to the studio, no one would see the fresh scar. But I also had gouges in my cheek and stitches next to my eye, so it would have been impossible for anyone not to notice. When Suki came up to me my first day back in class and asked me what had happened, I had to come clean. As it turned out, she didn't replace me, but she did tell me that I needed to take it easy and not push myself so that I could heal.

Between the stress of the injury and knowing that I had two important leading roles in the end-of-year workshop, the pressure was definitely getting to me. Although I never allowed it to show in my dancing, one of the ways that I dealt with my insecurities was by starting to eat more. It's not that I was sitting in my room and secretly stuffing myself, but because I was worried about spending money on food, I was eating things like pizza and macaroni salad. At the same time, I socialized more and went out with friends. Periodically we'd indulge ourselves by pigging-out on Entenmann's chocolate chip cookies and doughnuts. For the first time in my life, I was craving carbs—probably for their instant energy boost as well as their soothing properties. Later, when I was diagnosed with diabetes, controlling my carb cravings when my blood sugar was out of control would become a serious issue—but all that was still in the future. My weight gain, however, was not.

One morning, I was in class with Madame Tumkovsky (Tumi, to us students) and had just finished a series of pirouettes in a diagonal line across the room when she called me over and, in the middle of class, told me that Stanley wanted me to lose five pounds. I couldn't believe what I was hearing. It's not that either her message or her method of informing me was surprising; at the time, young dancers were often told to lose weight, and the message was rarely delivered in a warm or reassuring manner. But did she have to say it in front of the entire class?

I was immediately reminded of the first time I'd been humiliated by someone's criticism of my body. I was nine years old and in the fifth grade. The most popular boy in my class had blond hair and blue eyes and was so cool that he was going with a girl in the sixth grade, who happened to be one of Michele's best friends. I was delirious with joy when he wrote me a note in class that read, "You're a fox. You're cute." I couldn't believe he actually liked me.

At the end of the year my class had a Hawaiian luau where the girls danced in bathing suit tops and grass skirts. I was excited to have this cool guy see me dance, sure that he'd be impressed. I shook my hips just for him, and when the performance was over I went over to where he stood. Instead of complimenting me, however, he looked horrified and stared right at my chest.

"You're flat!" he said.

"What?" I asked.

"You're flat," he said again.

I made him repeat it a few more times while I tried to figure out what he meant. Did he mean I was skinny? Was he giving me a compliment? No, it couldn't have been a compliment, given the look of disgust on his face.

Once I got home, I pulled out the dictionary. Flat was defined as "level…without unevenness of surface as in tabletops…."

When I finally realized what he was talking about, I felt my face turning red. I was filled with shame. Until that moment it had never occurred to me to worry about whether someone would or wouldn't like me because of the way my body looked.

After that, there were no more notes from him. And, from then on, I wore loose sweatshirts over my clothes, even on the hottest days, which can be extremely hot in California.

Now, in Tumi's class, I once again felt deeply flawed and inadequate. Could I have been deluding myself into believing I was thin? Maybe I looked fat and just thought I was thin.

No dancer needs to be told how important it is to be thin. Balanchine, however, didn't expect his ballerinas to be emaciated. Although there was a body type he preferred, he was known to love dancers of all looks and sizes. He fell in love with a dancer's enthusiasm and passion, but, that being said, you did have to be as thin as your particular body could be. Personally, I had never had a problem staying thin, but now, for the first time, it wasn't so easy.

By the time that class ended, my head was spinning with contradictory thoughts. One moment I was planning how, from then on, I'd avoid food at all costs. The next moment I was telling myself that I'd simply cut out sweets and eat more healthfully; I wasn't going to turn into a neurotic, anorexic dancer just because Stanley wanted me to be perfect for his ballet.

On the one hand, I wanted to keep my perspective about food, but, at the same time, I was horrified at the prospect of not being what "they" wanted me to be. I started to eat less and to analyze every morsel of food I put in my mouth. I had never had a soft drink before, let alone a diet one, but now I started drinking Diet Coke instead of orange juice. After a long day of dancing, however, I'd find myself so hungry that I'd inevitably lose control and overeat—or, at least, eat more than I had wanted or intended to. Each time that happened I was overcome with guilt and em-barrassment, and terrified that my teachers would take away the roles I was dancing.

Naturally, I lost weight, and not surprisingly—given my per-sonality and control issues—I went too far. By the end of that year, I was being told I needed to gain a few pounds.

Despite the fear that my accident and short-lived weight gain would keep me from dancing them, I did perform both the Brahms and Stanley's Bournonville in the end-of-year workshop. I knew that Balanchine would be attending one of the final re-hearsals for his *Brahms-Schoenberg Quartet,* and the night before I was so excited I could hardly sleep.

By that time, Deidre and I had more or less gone our separate ways and found different groups of friends. My new roommate and best friend, Stacey, was a beautiful blonde who had quit ballet when she was sixteen to be a cheerleader, worked hard to get back in dancing shape, and been accepted for SAB's winter program at the very late age of eighteen. Stacey had a collection of beautiful leotards and dance skirts, and that night, she told me to borrow whichever ones I wanted for the next day's rehearsal. Since I couldn't sleep, anyway, I stayed up late trying on one after another until I finally chose a matching reddish-coral set.

Whenever Balanchine was rehearsing at SAB, everyone who was around came to watch. That day Peter Martins stood at the side barre while Jerome Robbins stood in the doorway; company members and SAB students lined the classroom walls. I was nervous but mostly excited; since we already had rehearsed so much, I was ready and surprisingly calm.

Stacey was a demi soloist in the same piece, and her part opened the ballet. She started with a series of big jumps and immediately fell flat on her face. We all looked at Balanchine. How was he going to react? As soon as he knew she wasn't hurt, he broke into a smile, and everyone in the room seemed to let their breath out at once. Stacey's fall had broken the tension and reminded everyone that Balanchine liked it when dancers fell because it meant they were going for it with all their energy.

In my pas de deux there was a sequence in which my partner walks toward me. It's a romantic moment, and my partner, James Sewell, wasn't doing it the way that Mr. B wanted him to.

"Be like man," Balanchine said, pounding his chest.

Jimmy tried, but he simply could not get the walk the way

Mr. B wanted it. Balanchine was known for being a great actor and a fine dancer who could demonstrate things precisely. Now he got up and walked toward me with his chest held high, taking firm steps and looking strong and powerful.

For a brief moment I was dancing with Mr. B.

I loved every moment of performing the Brahms, and the performances went well, even though I danced with injuries. One was the leg I'd hurt in the car accident and the other was a foot injury. Pain or no pain, nothing was going to stop me. The buzz was that Balanchine liked me, and I was fantasizing more than ever about a future with the New York City Ballet.

Shortly after the workshop performances, I graduated from PCS with a straight A average. I was sixteen years old. It felt great to know that I wouldn't have to worry about schoolwork anymore and could focus just on dance.

In July I went home for the summer, where my mom had all my favorite foods waiting: nectarines and plums and cashew nuts and bagels with lox and cream cheese. It was great to see Gent again. He still recognized my voice and gave me the neigh that I had so missed hearing. Romy, Michele, Mom, and I went for a great ride with all of our dogs through a beautiful forest opening onto a waterfall and a wide-open space where the horses could run and run. Even though I'd been gone for months, it didn't seem to matter; Gent and I were as connected as ever.

That summer I went folk dancing with my mom, camping with

my dad and Lynn, and ate as healthfully as I could. What I didn't tell anyone was how constantly I thought about the New York City Ballet and being thin enough for Balanchine.

In September, I returned to SAB.

I was seventeen, thin and ready to go.

FOURTEEN

The week I got back to New York I was once again called to Madame Gleboff's office along with my friend Stacey and one other student. Once more I received her news with mixed emotions, but this time my ambivalence had nothing to do with how I felt about pursuing a career with City Ballet. What Madame Gleboff told us was that Balanchine wanted us next for the company. But she quickly followed up that exciting news by cautioning us that Balanchine was ill. He was in the hospital, and there wouldn't be any new members taken that year, so if we had offers from other company directors who'd seen us in the workshop we should consider them. And, in any case, if Balanchine didn't recover, whoever took over might not choose us.

The three of us left her office in silence. Balanchine wanted us! But he was ill. He might not recover? I could not contemplate that possibility. Mr. B had been sick and in the hospital before and he'd always pulled through. I had to believe he'd pull through this time, as well.

* * *

Although no one wanted to imagine a City Ballet without Mr. B, we had often speculated among ourselves about who might take over on that faraway day when he was no longer around. People often suggested that it might be Peter Martins. I knew he'd cast me as a demi soloist and had chosen me to understudy the lead in his workshop performance of *The Magic Flute* my first year at SAB, so I was hoping he still liked me and would pick me for the company. But I wasn't even going to think about that because Balanchine would be fine. He had to be fine.

Meanwhile, classes and rehearsals continued as usual. For the workshop that year, Suki was staging two Balanchine ballets, *Valse-Fantaisie* and *Western Symphony.* I was chosen, along with two of my closest friends, Catherine and Kelly, to share the lead in *Valse Fantaisie,* each one dancing the part in one of the three times it would be performed. In addition, I was picked to dance the lead in one of the four movements of *Western Symphony.* My role was particularly meaningful to me because Balanchine had originally created it for his fourth wife, Tanaquil Le Clercq. It was sexy and flirtatious, requiring lots of energy, not to mention prancing on pointe, high kicks and lots of turning. In photographs, Tanny had always looked glamorous and sensual, qualities I had never attributed to myself. So when Suki invited a group of us to her home one evening to watch a video of the original cast, I was afraid that I'd be intimidated or discouraged by watching her. Instead, the opposite happened: Tanaquil's uninhibited, energetic and humorous performance made me realize that I could bring my own kind of energy and abilities to the role.

Now in my third year at SAB, I was working hard, loving the roles I was dancing and assuming, as we all were, that Balanchine would be at our final rehearsal for the workshop and at the performances as usual. At the same time, I was also enjoying more of a social life and forming close bonds with some of the other dancers. Although, on one level, we were competing with one another, on another level we inspired and supported one another. We knew that each one of us was unique, and we were hopeful that we would all be accepted into the company. We were extremely disciplined and danced all day under enormous pressure, but we were also very young, away from home, and, like any group of college-age students, we liked to let loose a bit in the evenings. We'd go out to dinner at one of the many local restaurants and occasionally we partied on weekends with guys from the men's advanced class and even a few from the company who occasionally showed up. My roommate, Stacey, made a mean daiquiri, so we would sometimes gather at our apartment to get drunk. And, of course, we also gossiped about who was dating whom in the company. Our "fun," however, always came second to the serious business of dancing.

Despite the outward appearance of normalcy, after several months of Balanchine's absence, it became clear that there was a real possibility he might never come back.

My friend and fellow student Peter Boal and I often talked

about visiting him. We felt a need to tell this man who had changed our lives just how much he had influenced us, how much he meant to us, and how much we missed him. At the same time, we worried that we might be intruding. After all, we were only students; we weren't even company members, and we really had no idea if he'd even know who we were. Finally, however, we decided we just had to go.

When we got to the hospital, we sat in the waiting room too nervous even to go up to the desk and ask if we could go in to see him. We were about to leave before we even entered the room when we heard a voice calling, "Come, come in." It was Karin von Aroldingen, a principal dancer with the company and Balanchine's closest companion at the time, and one of those who had been by his side throughout his illness. Karin told us that Balanchine was having a good day and that we should go in to see him.

Although he was very thin and pale, he seemed happy to see us and asked us to pull a couple of chairs up to his bedside, indicating that he had something to tell us.

Balanchine was passionate about many things, including art, dance, food and music, and we were sure that when he spoke his words would be both passionate and profound. Instead, he asked us if we were in school, and then talked for ten minutes about the importance of staying in school and getting a good academic education.

Normally, Balanchine did not condone anything that took his dancers' attention away from the theater; it didn't matter what it was: getting married, having a baby or going to college. His attitude generally was that if we wanted to go to school we could do it when we finished dancing.

Needless to say, Peter and I left the hospital confused. Why had Mr. B told us to stay in school? Was he thinking clearly, and if so, was he trying to tell us something about the future of the company without him?

Balanchine died April 30, 1983, the day of our first workshop performances. Lincoln Kirstein and Peter Martins announced his passing to the audience before the curtain went up, and we danced with more heart and soul than ever. It was the death of a genius and of an era.

His funeral, at the Cathedral of Our Lady of the Sign, a beautiful Russian Orthodox church on the east side of Manhattan, was attended by hundreds of people, many of whom comprised a history of dance in our century. As each of us entered the church, we were given a lighted candle, which we held, standing as is customary in Russian Orthodox churches, for what seemed like hours.

Standing at the very back of the church, I was spotted by Joseph Duell, the NYCB soloist who had choreographed a new work for the SAB workshop that I was in the first year I was there. Joe took my hand and led me closer to the front of the church. Karin Von Aroldingen, who was standing close by, nodded in my direction, as if to let me know that I was welcome and she was happy to see me there. I was touched that she and Joe seemed to think that I belonged.

When the service was over, we formed a long, long line and silently walked past the open casket to pay our last respects. Although I knew my grief couldn't compare to that of those who knew him so much better and who had worked with him every day, I, too, felt an inexpressible sorrow. I had been touched by Balanchine's greatness and the promise of a life working with him. Now I would never dance one of his new creations. I would not have the opportunity to be nurtured by his genius.

PART FOUR

After Balanchine and Before
Diabetes

FIFTEEN

That summer, I stayed in New York taking classes until August, then went home for a month to visit with my family. When I got back at the beginning of September, Madame Gleboff informed me, as well as Catherine and Kelly, that we were being made apprentices. I could apprentice for up to two years, during which time I would still be enrolled as a student at SAB. I would be expected to take company class, but I could take classes at SAB, as well, and perform in the end-of-year workshops. I could also perform in as many as three ballets with the company; if I performed in four they had to give me a full contract.

It goes without saying that what should have been one of the high points of my life was, in fact, extremely bittersweet because of the extreme devastation and grief being felt by the entire company.

Entering company class that fall was like arriving at Mount Olympus after Zeus had died, with a younger, less-experienced god now in charge and all the other gods feuding. Peter Martins and Jerome Robbins had both been named ballet masters in chief. Peter would be mainly responsible for artistic direction, and he would cast all the Balanchine ballets. Jerome Robbins would be responsible for casting his own ballets. Although I loved Peter and was thrilled that he would be in charge, not everyone was as happy as I was about Peter's promotion.

While Balanchine's general rule was that all his dancers study at SAB, Peter had been an exception since he was already an international star when he joined the company as a principal dancer in 1970. There were many dancers at NYCB who had worked with Balanchine far longer than Peter and who clearly resented taking direction from him.

In addition, there was a pervasive sense of uneasiness throughout the company. Balanchine never fired anyone; dancers who could no longer execute virtuoso steps were moved into character parts. Now no one knew if Peter would continue that policy. Beyond that, no one really knew whether or not Peter liked them, and as a result, dancers young and old were wondering whether they would continue to be cast in the roles they'd been dancing, or, in the worst case, asked to leave the company.

As it was when Balanchine was alive, company class was held in the main rehearsal hall on the fifth floor of the New York State Theater. When I entered for the first time, standing at the barres that lined the windowless walls, I saw dancers whom I'd watched onstage as an awestruck student at SAB. In addition to the members of the corps, there was Suzanne Farrell at one barre,

Merrill Ashley at another, along with Darci Kistler, Heather Watts and Ib Andersen. Everyone was following the usual preclass routine, stretching and working to get their muscles warmed up, but the air was thick with tension.

I couldn't help being nervous. It didn't help to remind myself that I'd worked at SAB with both Suzanne and Peter and that they liked me. I also wanted to be accepted by everyone in the company who had been Balanchine dancers. I wanted to prove to everyone that I was good enough to be there, that I would have been chosen by Balanchine, and that I wasn't there only because Peter had picked me.

Peter taught company class most mornings, and despite the air of uncertainty, everyone was professional and working hard. Everyone was there to dance, but we were all on shaky ground, and there was a palpable tension in the room. I felt as if I had been once again thrust into the midst of a dysfunctional family. The company was my family now. Everyone in the room was an authority figure to me, and I wanted them all to be okay both with the situation and with me—but the situation was not okay.

My guardian angel in those trying times turned out to be Joseph Duell. Joe knew that Peter Martins had far too much on his plate. On top of all of his new responsibilities as director and taking on the impossible task of trying to fill Balanchine's shoes, he was still performing and would have little time to guide new dancers. So, during what is called "center work," when we have finished our work at the barre and the class is divided into several groups, Joe took it upon himself to watch me, and after each combination he would give me incredibly helpful corrections.

In the midst of this difficult time for the company, I was chosen to perform my first role with New York City Ballet. I would be one of eight corps de ballet ladies who would dance behind four demi soloists and a leading couple in the fourth movement of Balanchine's *Symphony in C,* a classical "tutu ballet" with music by Georges Bizet. It was a perfect first ballet for me. There were no turns and no long balances, just quick movements and exuberant energy.

The night before my first performance, I was, of course, both nervous and excited. When the phone rang in the apartment I was sharing with Stacey, I figured my mom and Romy were calling to wish me good luck. My mom tried to sound normal but I could tell immediately that something wasn't right. I finally pried it out of her: Gent was dead. He had apparently fallen into a ditch and injured himself so badly that the vet had to put him down. She hadn't wanted to tell me, but she also knew that if she didn't call I'd know something was wrong, anyway, and maybe worry even more.

I was in shock and sick at heart. Gent was dead, and suddenly the anxiety I was feeling about my performance didn't seem very important. I needed to be a professional and learn to dance under any conditions, no matter what I might be feeling. I may have wanted to cancel the performance, but I knew I couldn't do that. It simply was not an option.

My feelings had never stopped me from dancing before; rather, dancing was what I had put my feelings *into.* The classroom and the stage were where I sorted through my emotions and found clarity through movement. Performing was where life made sense, where all the sorrow and uncertainties around me faded away.

When it came time to perform the next evening, my grief was transformed, and I reveled in every step I took on the stage—a pattern that was to continue throughout my professional life.

SIXTEEN

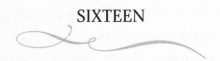

At the end of my first season as an apprentice, in June 1984, I was made a full member of the corps de ballet. I had just turned eighteen. I went from taking two classes a day and rehearsing for one workshop performance at the end of the year, to taking an hour-and-a half morning class, rehearsing up to six hours a day, and doing eight performances over the course of a six-day week.

In the winter season, which runs from November to March, the company would be dancing at least forty-five ballets and perhaps as many as seventy-five or more. As a new member of the corps, I would dance in many of them. When I was preparing for a workshop at SAB, I'd had a month or so to learn a new ballet and many more months to perfect it. Now I was learning and performing entire ballets in a matter of days.

The ballets were taught and rehearsed by Rosemary Dunleavy, who was the main ballet mistress. I was amazed at the way she could literally remember every person's part in every ballet—all the counts steps, and intricate patterns. And she did it without looking at notes or a video. It was mind-blowing.

Rosemary taught clearly and concisely and made it easy to learn. We spent entire days in the studio with her, and she was the one who would choose which corps dancers would be featured. She noticed that I was a quick study and seemed to like me. I was lucky, because Rosemary was the one who cast the members of the corps. If she liked you, she could give you choice corps roles; if she didn't, she could also make sure you didn't get them. Or, even worse, she could see to it that you didn't dance very much at all.

Some rehearsals were to learn new parts; others were final orchestra and costume rehearsals for the ballet that would be danced that evening. The corps, soloists and principals each rehearsed separately to learn their parts and the technique of a particular work. The entire ballet was often not put together until the final rehearsal—literally hours before it was to be performed.

Evening performances began at 8:00 p.m. After I'd applied my makeup, I would change into my performance pink tights, and put on my warm-up clothes—leg warmers, parachute pants and a zippered parka—and stretch. If I wasn't in the first piece, I liked to warm up at one of the backstage barres so that I could see what was happening onstage.

Ballets choreographed by Jerome Robbins, Mr. B or Peter Martins generally run twenty to forty minutes, with a full night's program comprised of three or four of them. One of the best things about being in the corps of City Ballet was that we danced as much as the soloists. In many classical ballets, members of the corps pose more than they dance, but in Balanchine's plotless pieces, we danced a lot and we danced hard. It was incredibly exciting and exhilarating, but it was also exhausting and made for a pretty grueling schedule. I had to learn to pace myself. It took time to figure out how to dance full out during morning class, again in rehearsals, and still hold something back for the performance itself.

What I found was that the sheer excitement of being onstage—the lights, the costumes, the music, the power of the choreography and the energy of other dancers—brought me to a level of energy I never dreamed I had. Although Balanchine was gone, his spirit was alive in his ballets, the teachers, his dancers and all those who had worked so closely with him. At many performances, Lincoln Kirstein was seated in the first row of the first balcony, and even though it was difficult to see particular faces in the audience, I could always see Lincoln, and I could feel his larger-than-life presence.

After performances, no matter how tired I was, how much my feet hurt or how much I was craving sleep, my mind would not turn off and I'd lie in bed humming the music of the last piece I'd danced or going over the steps I would dance the next day. Sleep had never come easy for me. As a little girl in Thailand, I'd often awaken in terror in the middle of the night and not be able to go back to sleep. Now my inability to get a full night's sleep was due in part to sheer excitement and in part to overexhaustion and a racing mind.

The same year I joined the company, Romy, who was by then fifteen years old, received a scholarship to the winter program at SAB. When she first arrived, I was still living with Stacey, so she shared a room with my friend Catherine in another apartment in the same building. But when Stacey decided to move out on her own, it seemed natural that Romy and I would find a place we could share. More than just sisters, we were becoming best friends, and now, when I got home after a performance, I knew she'd be there waiting to talk. I still had trouble sleeping, but having her there made me feel calm and safe, and eventually I'd doze off.

SEVENTEEN

My first review was in *Dance* magazine and was written by Joan Acocella, who would go on to become the dance critic for *The New Yorker*. "Zippora Karz, who always looks shiny and clean— as if she were going to a party and her mother just did her braids—glows visibly from whatever corner of the corps she's occupying. One always sees her, hails her, loves her go-for-it eagerness. She seems ready to eat the entire repertoire," Acocella wrote. Even though I was a bit embarrassed to be described as some kind of super-scrubbed Goody Two-shoes, it felt great to be singled out.

I was hungry for the feedback because, while at SAB, I had always received corrections and constructive criticism after every rehearsal and in every class, it was different in the company. The person responsible for the corps was Rosemary, who had many dancers to watch and tend to and who was not, in any case, inclined to stroke us. Corrections from Rosemary were rare and came only if we were visibly out of step or doing something obviously wrong.

Her compliments, on the other hand, were so infrequent that I still remember the one occasion when she came to the corps dressing room as eight of us, seated along one side of the table, were removing our makeup after a performance. She said, "That was excellent, girls! Nice job." After she left, one of the other dancers turned to us and asked, "Who are you and what have you done with Rosemary?" We all cracked up laughing.

The next "first" for me was a big one—dancing a leading role in *The Nutcracker.* Every ballet company needs to raise money, and most of them, including City Ballet, rely on the revenue from their annual performances of *The Nutcracker.* Balanchine choreographed his own version in 1954, and it soon became the company's custom to perform it exclusively from Thanksgiving until after New Year's Day—to sold-out houses for every performance. In fact, the proceeds from *The Nutcracker* financed everything else we danced in the course of a season.

The first time I had danced it as an apprentice, I was given two roles in the first act: the maid in the opening party scene, which was actually a nondancing part, and a snowflake that appears on the journey to the Land of the Sweets. Being a snowflake definitely had its hazards.We all held pom-poms in both hands as we danced, and one girl's pom-poms would often get entangled with another's, at which point there would be a silent battle for who was going to hold on to her pom-poms and who was going to let go. And then, as the Snowflakes danced, the prop people scattered little paper snowflakes onto the stage. During intermission, they swept up the snowflakes to be reused at the next show. This meant that as a snowflake, you could get hit on the head by an errant earring or hairpin that had been swept up after the previous performance.

One night, during my second *Nutcracker* season, I was at the resin box during intermission, securing my toe shoes for my second-act appearance in the "Waltz of the Flowers," when Rosemary came over to me, whispered that Peter wanted me to watch the pas de deux, and walked away. I wasn't sure I had heard her correctly. There are many pas de deux in *The Nutcracker,* but only one that was ever referred to as "the" pas de deux. Was that really the one she wanted me to watch?

The grand pas de deux, danced by the Sugar Plum Fairy and her cavalier, which comes after all the other characters in the Land of Sweets have danced, is the grand climax of the entire ballet. The Tchaikovsky music starts softly as the Sugar Plum Fairy, wearing a light green tutu and being led by her cavalier, begins the dance. That evening, after I had danced in the "Waltz of the Flowers," I stepped into the wing and watched my idol, Suzanne Farrell, partnered by Adam Luders. Their dancing was majestic and romantic, and I watched them in awe. This couldn't have been the dance Rosemary meant me to watch. I couldn't possibly be ready to dance it.

Each night, after the final rehearsal of the day, we dancers went to our dressing rooms to put on our makeup, and Rosemary went to her office to work out the schedule, which listed where each of the company's one hundred or so dancers needed to be at every moment of the following day. Only Rosemary's famously computerlike brain could figure this out.

The schedule was posted during the evening's performance, so we never knew in advance what it would be. On this particular night we all gathered around as usual to see what tomorrow would bring, and there it was. Usually my name was posted with numerous other names for a corps rehearsal with Rosemary. Now, according to the schedule, Peter Boal, my friend from SAB, and I were to rehearse *The Nutcracker.* In the section of the schedule that tells you who your rehearsal mistress or master will be, I saw the name Peter Martins. Everyone knew that Peter Martins only rehearsed dancers in principal roles. So it was true; Rosemary *had* meant "the" pas de deux. Balanchine was famous for plucking dancers from the corps to perform leading roles, and now Peter was doing the same for me. I was excited, overwhelmed, embarrassed and uncomfortable all at once. Would I live up to his expectations? How would the other dancers who had danced the part for Balanchine feel about my performing it now? I was still as concerned about being accepted by the rest of the company as I was about my ability to excel.

Most dancers, at some point in their training, are taught the solos for *The Nutcracker.* Luckily, I had learned the choreography for the Sugar Plum Fairy from Suki at SAB, and Peter Boal and I both knew the choreography for the grand pas de deux.

When you learn a leading role for a workshop as a student, you try not to fantasize about performing leads as a member of the company. But dancing Sugar Plum on the stage of the State Theater was the dream for all of us. So when I read the schedule that night, it seemed like a dream come true—not only because I'd been called to learn Sugar Plum, but also because it meant that Peter was thinking of me as someone who could dance leading roles.

When I got to rehearsal the next day, Peter Martins was already there, and Suzanne Farrell was watching from the wings. Peter went through the entire pas de deux with us, correcting every step and giving countless directions. Because not only was he a danseur noble (literally a "noble dancer"), he was also one of the greatest partners of all time, we both naturally savored every direction and correction he gave us. Balanchine didn't want the man nervously hovering behind his ballerina, looking as if he were waiting to grab her. The man was to stand at a distance and come in at the last possible second, gently gliding his hand around his ballerina's waist for a turn or a jump. The audience shouldn't notice him. I'd watched Peter perform this magical "disappearing act" numerous times with Suzanne and his other partners. Now the directions he gave Peter Boal were based on the idea that in certain parts of the pas de deux, a good partner will make himself as invisible as possible, presenting his ballerina so beautifully that the audience's focus is entirely on her.

And all the while Peter worked with us, Suzanne watched silently from the wings.

For us, just rehearsing with Peter Martins was incredibly

special and signified what he had in mind for our futures, but neither of us dared to speculate about whether or not we'd actually be cast to dance our roles in a performance. The next day, casting was posted for the following week. And there we were, cast as the Sugar Plum Fairy and her cavalier in Balanchine's *The Nutcracker.*

It was absolutely unbelievable, and we had less than a week to prepare. In most companies, principal roles are cast weeks or even months in advance, but at City Ballet, it was always one week before. As we continued to rehearse the pas de deux with Peter Martins, Suzanne continued to look on.

For the solo, I worked with Rosemary, who picked the role apart, giving me notes on every single step. Her corrections included what to do with my hands, my feet, my head, even my pinkie finger. Rosemary was a great technician and I learned an enormous amount from her, but I was getting overwhelmed by the details. I felt so pressured to be technically perfect that I couldn't focus on the nuances of phrasing, musicality and the feeling of the work, all of which, in combination with technical brilliance, are what allow one to give a magical performance.

Suzanne had always made me feel that I didn't have to adhere to anyone else's preconceived idea of perfection, and I needed her help and her attitude now. One day, I asked if she would come to the studio with me for fifteen minutes. A great dancer does not necessarily make a great coach, but I trusted Suzanne and knew she would know just how to guide me. She was becoming my Balanchine.

Suzanne taught as she danced—from the heart. She could see that all the pressure was taking a toll on my expressiveness and musicality—the very qualities that had prompted Peter Martins to cast me in the role and two of the most important qualities any ballerina can bring to the stage—and she wasn't happy. "Go home and listen to the music," she told me. "Close your eyes and see yourself dancing. Feel the music. Feel the dance. See it." Her words were inspiring and comforting. When I got home I put on my Walkman and dimmed the lights, but the visualization wasn't easy for me. The first few times I tried to see myself dancing as I listened to Tchaikovsky's score, I saw myself falling down. At that point I would stop the music, quiet my fear and do it again—over and over until I could see myself dancing the steps the way I dreamed of doing them. I also tried to see myself enjoying the role and, most important, dancing it from my heart. Hundreds of visualizations later, I saw a flawless performance in which I embodied Tchaikovsky's music with passion and soul, just like Suzanne.

In the few days remaining before the performance, I tried to stay calm. During the day I was so busy rehearsing that I didn't have time to get caught up in my anxiety. In the evenings, I was busy dancing my usual parts as a snowflake, a marzipan shepherdess and occasionally a flower in *The Nutcracker*. But trying to sleep at night was hopeless. Romy talked to me until she had to close her eyes, and when I finally dozed off my anxiety manifested in disturbing dreams.

The night before the performance, I dreamed that I was

standing at the top of an icy mountain with my skis on. The slope was so steep that the mountain dropped straight down in front of me. As I made my way toward the perilously steep slope, I realized I didn't know how to ski. Then I realized that I was completely naked. That's how I felt: totally exposed and vulnerable, unprepared to tackle what I was about to do, and out of my element. But frightened or not, with or without sleep, the performance would go on.

My mother came to New York for my first solo performance along with Sheila and two other teachers from her studio, Chris and Marilee, who had always been my great supporters. I was afraid that having them there would add to the pressure I felt, but it actually helped knowing they were in the audience, and I was glad they had come.

Peter Boal and I were nervous and shaky as we stood in the wings like third graders before a big school play. From the other side of the back stage area Heather Watts and Jock Soto waved to us, wishing us good luck. Dancers in a ballet company have a rare camaraderie. There are rivalries, of course, and while I knew some of the others were upset that they hadn't been chosen, I felt incredibly supported by everyone. We are like a team, and when each of us is dancing our best, the team as a whole is lifted to a higher level of performance.

All of our training and rehearsing pays off in the performance, that moment when, despite whatever nerves you might feel, your mind and body take over, you focus on the moment and you just let go. When the performance began that night, something took over inside us. The turns I kept falling off of when I began visualizing now went beautifully. The more we danced the freer we became. When it ended, what made me most happy was that despite the pressure and my fear that I wasn't ready, I had been able to get my mind out of the way and dance from my heart. At moments it felt as if I had allowed something greater and grander than myself to be expressed through me.

Afterward, Peter Martins would describe his impression of my performance to Sheila in three words, "Simple, pure and unaffected." Clive Barnes, reviewing in the *New York Post,* wrote, "Both Karz, a controlled yet exultant dancer, with a rhapsodic, flowing line and beautiful placing that punctuates her dance with split-frozen seconds of sculpture, and the elegant Boal, showed a great deal more than promise. These two are potential stars."

Joe Duell came up to me onstage immediately after the performance, hugged me and said, "This is your home."

EIGHTEEN

Right after my performance in the grand pas de deux, I went back to rehearsing my usual corps de ballet roles. After one of those rehearsals the following week, Rosemary called me aside and said, "I know that Sugar Plum was a big deal for you and you danced well, but it will probably be a while before you dance anything that big again. I don't want you to get depressed about it. For now, you should work on getting technically stronger."

Getting that kind of feedback from Rosemary was unusual, and I appreciated it. More often, you aren't told why you're not being cast again; the roles just go to other dancers. And, in any case, I knew that I needed to get stronger. So long as I was being considered for principal roles in the future, I could wait. In the meanwhile, I was performing every night in ballets that were challenging and inspiring and would help me develop the strength I required.

As it turned out, however, I didn't have to wait as long as I'd anticipated. Jerome Robbins always had an eye out for new talent, and he had come to see my *Nutcracker* performance. I obviously made an impression, because a few weeks later he chose me to dance a lead in his epic ballet *The Goldberg Variations,* set to the music of Johann Sebastian Bach. He'd originally choreographed the role for Gelsey Kirkland, one of the world's greatest ballerinas. I was surprised and extremely grateful that he had noticed me and chosen me for the part.

After I'd rehearsed the part with ballet mistress Sally Leland, Jerry said that he wanted to rehearse me in my solo himself. The idea of dancing for Jerry was exciting, of course, but also terrifying.

Since Balanchine's death, Jerome Robbins was the living genius and master choreographer for City Ballet, producing amazing works all the time. Watching his ballets evoked in me the same depth of feeling I experienced watching Balanchine ballets. But while Balanchine was a kindly, endlessly patient presence, Jerry was unpredictable, unsettling and utterly intimidating. His volatile temper was famous throughout the dance world. There is a well-known story of an incident that occurred when, years earlier, he was directing *Billion Dollar Baby.* He had been yelling at the cast, and as he verbally tore into them, he kept backing up slowly but surely toward the orchestra pit. The entire cast saw what was happening but no one said a word. Instead, everyone stood silently by as Jerry fell backward into the pit, injuring himself quite severely, and nobody had tried to stop it.

But working with Jerry was worth it. He could push, mold and inspire a performer to achieve his or her highest potential. And even he had a sweet, gentle side, and when he was nice, the whole room lit up. Everyone was happy when Jerry was happy, and everyone—including me—wanted to be part of whatever he was creating.

The rehearsal for my solo in *Goldberg* was the first time I had ever been alone with Jerry. I had started to dance the beautiful piano piece when suddenly I hit a slippery spot on the floor and I fell flat on my face. It took me a second to realize what had happened. And when I looked up at Jerry, expecting him to ask if I was okay, he yelled, "Get up!"

I was flat on my stomach and getting up wasn't easy. I tried but couldn't. Again, Jerry yelled, "Get up!" A moment later he yelled louder, then still louder. *"Get up! Get up!"* Finally, I managed to get back on my feet, brushed the dirt off my stomach and started again where I'd left off.

Much as I wanted Jerry to like me, much as I hoped he'd be inspired by me and one day nurture me as I'd hoped Balanchine would have done, I really wished he weren't so mean and temperamental.

With the promise of dancing a lead for Jerry and future leads for Peter, I took Rosemary's advice to heart and did whatever I could to increase my muscle strength. "Be strong" had become my constant mantra. I was obsessed with working my body as hard as was humanly possible, adding Pilates, weight lifting and yoga to my already intense schedule. In class, during our center work, instead of resting like most of the others while the second group danced, I danced with both groups. I wanted to be strong enough and consistent enough to dance leading roles. Overall, however, I was happy. I was no longer nervous in company class and I loved performing every night. It seemed to me that I was much further along than I had even dreamed of being at this point.

Just one thing was really bothering me. Joe Duell had suddenly stopped correcting me in company class. When I said hello as I passed him in the hall, he stared blankly ahead and ignored me. Now I wondered if I'd done something wrong. Was Joe disappointed in me?

This was particularly upsetting because Joe had always been there, correcting me in class, saying hello in the hall, and once, when he saw that I was struggling, he even asked me to lunch. Back in the fall, before I'd been chosen to dance Sugar Plum, the company had gone to Washington, D.C., to perform at the Kennedy Center. I loved the experience of seeing new places, performing for new audiences and bonding with the other company members in ways that you don't when you're not on the road. But on that particular tour, the lack of feedback had really gotten to me. I was feeling particularly insecure and even a bit depressed. As usual Joe Duell noticed and suggested that we go to lunch. Even though I'd never had a problem talking to people, I was nervous. Could I tell Joe what I was feeling? I knew that Peter and Rosemary had the entire company of dancers to think about, and I didn't want to complain or seem ungrateful. I don't remember what we talked about at that lunch, and in the end, I'm not sure it really mattered. It was enough that Joe had taken the time from his busy schedule to be sure I was okay.

But I do remember that something very odd happened at that lunch. A fly kept landing on Joe's forehead. It kept circling around, and I kept waiting for him to swat it, but he didn't. At one point, while he was eating, it actually flew onto his lip, and still he did nothing. As he continued to speak, it stayed there. I tried to listen to what he was saying, but all I could focus on was the fly on his lip. How strange, I thought. He didn't notice it.

I thought of that incident now as I worried about the change in his behavior. I had enough self-awareness to realize that because of my own insecurities, I was making this all about me. But what if his problem had nothing to do with me? I always knew when something was bothering my friends, and I was always able to reach out to them. So why couldn't I reach out to him? I vowed to myself that the next time the opportunity arose, I was going to ask him how he was doing. He could tell me or not, but at least I'd have made the effort—as he had for me in Washington.

Every day I'd look for a chance to speak with him alone, but he'd become elusive. Then one day we were waiting for the elevator together—just the two of us. I kept telling myself that this was my chance, but I just couldn't do it. I froze, and I didn't know why. If he'd given me the slightest opening, I might have mustered up the courage, but although we were standing next to each other, it was as if I wasn't even there with him.

The next day, during stage rehearsal for *Symphony in C,* I sat at the very front of the stage with Stacey and the other dancers, waiting to rehearse our parts while Joe rehearsed his. As we sat there watching him dance, I whispered to Stacey how concerned I was about him. She took me by the hand and whispered back, "Something's not right. I can't look at him. He seems all cold and clammy."

The day after that, while we were in the dressing room getting ready for a matinee performance of *A Midsummer Night's Dream,* an announcement came over the loudspeaker: "All dancers come to stage level immediately."

Everyone froze for an instant and then rushed to the elevator. The last time that announcement had been made to the company, it was to announce Balanchine's death. Something was terribly wrong and everyone could feel it. Some of the older corps women burst into tears, thinking that Lincoln Kirstein must have passed away.

The elevator was too small to accommodate everyone at once, and when I finally arrived at the stage level the first person I saw was Lincoln, towering above everyone else in the middle of the stage. Then I heard screams and gasps. Everyone looked shocked and horror-struck as they fell sobbing into one another's arms.

I found Catherine Oppenheimer, one of the last women Balanchine had taken into the company, standing off to the side, tears streaming down her face. "Joe killed himself," she said.

He had jumped out the window of his fifth-floor apartment. He was twenty-nine years old, and I could only imagine the kind of pain he must have been in to do such a thing. I couldn't believe it.

He had been scheduled to dance that matinee. As always, the show went on.

NINETEEN

Luckily, there was only one week left in the season, because after Joe's death I was finding it more and more difficult to keep going. Instead of warming up my muscles before the performance, I sat in a chair feeling as if I were stuck in mud. On Mondays—our day off—I generally did errands, cleaned the apartment and sometimes took a yoga class. On the Monday after Joe's death, I sat in bed all day staring at the TV.

The last day of the season, Lincoln, Peter and Jerry called a company meeting. I knew that Lincoln had been especially close to Joe, and the loss must have been terrible for him. Now the three of them told us that they understood what a horrible time this had been. They wanted us to go away and rest, and not to think about ballet during our two weeks off. In effect, they were giving us permission to let down and fall apart. I felt that I already had. Now, with their blessing, I went home and didn't think about ballet for two weeks.

* * *

For some dancers who are in peak condition, a two-week break will not drastically affect their form; I wasn't one of them. When we returned after the break, I had lost muscle response, particularly in my toes. I wasn't yet ready to take on a full schedule. I needed time to get back into shape mentally and physically, but I didn't have that luxury.

During the first week of rehearsals for the spring season, Jerry picked me to learn the only pas de deux in his playful work *Interplay*. When Jerry really liked a dancer, he wanted her for everything, and soon I was also learning a leading role in his masterpiece *Dances at a Gathering*.

For *Interplay*, I was to be third cast understudy, which meant that during rehearsals I could stand behind the other soloist and principal dancers while I tried to get myself back into shape. One day that first week, however, Jerry surprised us by showing up unannounced at rehearsal. We were still learning our parts, and I was still struggling to find my toes again. So, when Jerry said that he wanted to see all the casts for the pas de deux, I knew I wasn't ready. I looked at the clock and I prayed that we would run out of time before he got to me. But luck was not on my side, and to my dismay, there was just enough time left for me to dance.

When it was over, I knew that I hadn't done well. Actually, I was surprised that I had done as well as I did. Still, considering how good it needed to be for Jerry, it was pretty bad.

"You'll see," one of the older corps members had recently

warned me. "One day you're in and the next you're out. It will happen to you, too. Jerry does that." While I appreciated her attempt to prepare me for what had happened to her, I was secretly thinking that it would be different for me. Now I couldn't believe that one less-than-perfect rehearsal would cause him to drop me. Soon enough, however, I discovered how right she had been.

The Goldberg Variations was to be staged again toward the end of the season. Since Jerry had been pleased enough with my performance to then choose me for *Interplay*, I was naturally assuming that I would be cast again. When I asked Sally Leland if I should start thinking about rehearsing it on my own so I would be ready when Jerry wanted to see it, she smiled and put her hand on my shoulder. "Don't worry about rehearsing it," she said. "He's going to use somebody else."

The next day, when I looked at the rehearsal schedule, I saw that a younger corps member had been cast in the role. At twenty years old, I was already a has-been and I felt incredibly rejected. I knew I hadn't danced well in the rehearsal for *Interplay*, but I still didn't expect to be canned so quickly. I was heartbroken. I didn't want to accept it.

A few weeks later, I was rehearsing a corps de ballet role in yet another of Jerry's ballets, *In G Major*, when, as I was coming down from a jump, I lost focus for a split second. My foot twisted. I limped away. It turned out that I had broken my metatarsal and sprained my ankle. That put an end to my spring season, and I flew home to Los Angeles with my foot in a cast.

* * *

I was home for three months and gave myself permission to relax. I went to fraternity parties with my older sister, Michele, and her friends, got drunk and actually went on a few dates. It was a relief to be a normal twenty-year-old, to be around people who knew nothing about executing a perfect *tendu,* and who hadn't even heard of Jerry Robbins.

It was also the perfect time to heal the grief I'd been feeling ever since Joe's death, and to reflect on the feelings of rejection Jerry had triggered in me.

My aunt Rhonda had become a trainer for a program called the Loving Relationships Training, which, like many such programs in the eighties, focused on the notion that our thoughts create our reality, and that by becoming aware of our unconscious thoughts and changing them, we can change our reality. My mom and I took the course together, and it turned out to be an opportunity for us to heal some of our issues—specifically what had happened with Dave—and a powerful bonding experience for the two of us.

Taking those seminars taught me how much my sense of self-worth was directly related to whether or not Jerry and Peter were pleased with me. I realized I had a lot to work on. For my mother, the whole experience was so liberating that she decided to enroll in a six-month course that met weekly in New York. And so, at the end of the summer, she joined Romy and me in the city.

TWENTY

Back in New York City in late summer, I'd recovered from my injury and was using the time before rehearsals for the winter season began to get myself back in shape for dancing. I was spending a lot of time taking yoga classes at the White Cloud Studio. Julio Horvath, the owner, was just developing a new system he called Gyrotonics, which was designed to elongate and strengthen the muscles. Julio, born in Hungary, had dark hair and fire in his eyes and had once been a dancer himself. Now he was inspired by those of us from City Ballet, whose strong, flexible, athletic bodies allowed us to do extraordinary things.

I'd been dragged to Julio's studio by Sabrina, a beautiful long-legged dancer who came from Texas, and when I saw how much Julio's techniques were helping my dancing, I dragged Romy and Stacey there, too. Soon there was a big group of New York City Ballet dancers breathing, making grunting noises and putting our bodies in all kinds of contortionist positions as we worked with Julio.

Even though my ankle injury had healed, when I danced too much it still bothered me, so when someone from the yoga studio organized a group to consult a medicine man from the Philippines who called himself a psychic surgeon, I was happy to go along. At least a hundred people, including Romy, Stacey, Sabrina and I, showed up to get miraculously "healed." When my name was called, I entered a room furnished with a massage table and smelling of rubbing alcohol. A sweet-looking Philippine woman stood next to a small table that held a dishpan of water and cloths. She handed me a robe and asked me to put it on. Then she motioned to the healer, who had been standing close by. He couldn't have been over forty and was about my height, with dark hair and a twinkle in his eye. Now he motioned for me to lie down on the massage table.

As I lay on my back, the woman sprinkled the rubbing alcohol on my stomach. The medicine man put his fingertips on my torso and started moving them quickly, as if he were digging in the sand. He clasped one hand tight, appearing to grab something from inside my body, which he then lifted in the air and dangled in my face. It looked like a raw chicken liver or some kind of intestines. Then he went back for "more." He continued this process, working on different parts of my body—my hips, knees and my ankle. As he was digging, I felt a tiny pull, but that was about all.

Each time he supposedly pulled something out of me, he dangled it in my face and laughed. "You see," he said. "You see."

I wasn't sure if he was for real or not, and I was trying to figure out how he did it. Maybe the little chicken-liver-like things had been in his hand before he started digging. I tried to watch his every move to see if I could catch him. It struck me that he was way too showy, and I wondered if he were a scam artist. Then suddenly his face turned serious and his eyes pierced into mine. "You need to see me more," he said.

"Why?" I asked. His sudden change of manner made me curious.

"There is a problem in your blood," he answered.

I looked at him. He seemed genuinely concerned. Momentarily chilled, I quickly dismissed what he'd said and forgot all about it until I was diagnosed with diabetes about four months later.

As rehearsals began, the word was that Peter Martins was choreographing a new ballet to premiere toward the end of February. I would have loved just to be in the corps of Peter's new ballet, but I had no idea when—if ever—he would want to work with me again. He hadn't seen me dance since my injury, and it was possible that he didn't even know I was back.

Each night, I checked the rehearsal schedule for the next day, and finally, there was my name, listed with Peter Boal's for a rehearsal with Peter Martins for his new ballet. I'd been chosen to dance a lead. I was thrilled. I couldn't believe it.

The new piece, *Les Petits Riens,* would be choreographed for eight young corps de ballet members: four women and four men. Each couple would dance a pas de deux and each dancer would have a solo.

To have Peter Martins create a role for me was yet another dream come true. It's both a tribute and a challenge: a tribute in the sense that you've been chosen because the choreographer is inspired by something about you, and a challenge because even though choreographers make use of their dancers' strengths, they also like to push their dancers to confront their weaknesses. Balanchine was known to push dancers all the time. Once he even went so far as to have created a ballet that consisted almost entirely of jumps for a dancer he liked who had difficulty jumping. Peter, who was most inspired by athleticism, also loved to challenge dancers. His choreography could look extremely simple, but when done right it took incredible strength and control. Knowing this, I was worried that, even though I was back from my injury, I wouldn't be strong enough to do what he required.

The first day of rehearsal, Peter, looking godlike as usual in his white jeans and white sneakers, listened to the pianist play the first chords over and over, while he looked at me standing next to him, as if he were thinking, "Hmm, what is her body telling me I should do with her?" One of the steps I still had problems executing consistently was a really clean, perfect turn. So what did Peter do? He gave me a turn that required absolutely perfect balance.

Whenever Peter taught or rehearsed us, he demonstrated with perfect technique. Now he took a fifth position and did a pirouette, which is a turn on one leg with the other leg bent and its foot placed just under the knee. As he finished the pirouette, he did something absolutely amazing. Usually, when you finish a turn, both feet return to the ground, which is what stops your momentum. Now, instead of putting his bent leg on the floor, he opened it to the side and somehow stopped the turn while still standing on demi pointe on one foot. Finally, he lowered the raised leg and placed it, still in the air, near the back of the standing ankle. He did all of this slowly and with perfect control. Then he looked at me, indicating that I was to do the same thing, but on pointe. I didn't think, I just went for it, and as beginner's luck would have it, it worked.

I think we were both surprised. So Peter, excited by how well I had done it, decided to have me do it a second time—two of those incredibly difficult turns right at the beginning of my solo. What had I got myself into? How on earth would I re-create that step perfectly at each rehearsal, let alone at every performance?

In addition to preparing for *Les Petits* I was rehearsing all my other corps parts every day and performing every night. There simply wasn't any time to pay attention to what my body was trying to tell me. I don't know when the constant thirst, the frequent trips to the bathroom, the burning hunger and the spaced-out feeling had started, but I attributed my symptoms to being stressed and tired and ignored them all. If it hadn't been for the painful sores under my arms, I don't know if I ever would have gone to the doctor.

The week of the premiere we had orchestra and costume rehearsals for *Petits*. My physical problems seemed small compared to my nerves, and I willed myself to focus and stay centered so that I could nail my difficult steps. In one dress rehearsal I kept falling off pointe. All I had to do was hold an arabesque while Peter Boal walked around me as he held my waist and I held his shoulder. It was one of the easiest steps in our dance and shouldn't have been a problem, but no matter how hard I tried, I couldn't stay on pointe. I was furious with my body for screwing up at this crucial time, and I couldn't figure out what the problem was; nerves was not a valid excuse.

I could see Peter Martins growing more and more tense as he watched me mess it up. Any new work is of vital importance to its choreographer, and this was especially true for Peter, who, as the new director, had the entire ballet world watching him. Now, as he looked at me, he frowned and turned to Susie Hendl, the ballet mistress who had been rehearsing me for the part—the same Susie Hendl who had auditioned me and given me the scholarship to SAB. "What's wrong with her, Susie?" he asked. "Why can't she do it?"

I vowed that I wasn't going to let my body rob me of this great experience. I knew how to perform. I would muster up whatever I needed to get through all six performances of *Les Petit Riens*. In the end, I didn't think I was all that great, but I did manage to dance well. Except for the moment when I saw Jerry walking away from the wing during my solo, I was happy to be on the stage.

TWENTY-ONE

Once the performances of *Les Petits Riens* were over and I'd gone back to dancing my regular corps roles, I had expected that I would start to feel better. But I was wrong.

Once I had a diagnosis, as much as I was in denial about my illness, I couldn't deny that there was *something* seriously wrong with me and that I could not continue to perform feeling the way I did.

With only two weeks left of the season I'd told Rosemary that I could not dance. I didn't want to be in New York anymore. I didn't want to know about the performances I would be missing; I didn't want to have to explain myself to anyone. If I couldn't be part of that world, I just wanted to be as far away from it as possible. But I couldn't leave immediately. I'd have to go back to the theater at least one more time to clear my things out of the dressing room we'd be vacating until our spring season began so that the City Opera could move in.

And I also had to tell my mother what was going on. I'd already confided in Romy the night before, but I knew that telling my mom was going to be harder—for both of us. I didn't want her sympathy, because I still didn't want to believe this was happening to me. I also knew she'd be upset, and I didn't want to have to deal with her emotions when I didn't know how to deal with my own.

When I finally told her, she took a deep breath and sighed, then gave me a look that seemed to be a combination of half worried and half sad. She said nothing. I was shocked by her silence, but I suppose I shouldn't have been. When my mother didn't know what to say, she said nothing, and this was clearly one of those times. She tried to put her arms around me, but I pushed her away. I didn't want sympathy and I didn't want anyone to touch me.

Word began to spread, and of course my friends found out. They tried to be there for me when they could, but they were at the theater all day and all night. Stacey bought me a teddy bear that she said had diabetes, too; Catherine called to see if I needed anything. I appreciated their concern, but there really wasn't anything they could do. And I still didn't want to talk about it, especially when they were calling during a five-minute break and I could hear music playing in the background for a rehearsal I wanted to be at more than anything.

For my part, I was packing my things, booking a flight to L.A. and trying to stay focused on what I needed to do. In the midst of all this, I decided to call my aunt Rhonda. At the time, I'd been able to share my emotions with her in a way that I couldn't with my mother. I hoped that as a counselor for people going through hardships, Rhonda would be able to counsel me, too.

Instead of providing the comfort I was seeking, though, this is what she said: "I think you're creating this because you want your father's attention. He's a doctor, so this is a good way to get it." I appreciated her concern and her belief that I could get through the disease once I'd uncovered the unconscious thought pattern that had caused it, but her words only left me feeling angry and even more alone. The same belief system that had previously made me feel that I had control over a given situation—the conviction that I could change it—offered no solace now. In the midst of my shock, denial and overwhelming emotions, the notion that I had in any way contributed to my illness brought no sense of empowerment, only more devastation. I felt like the ultimate failure—spiritually, emotionally and physically.

What I could see was that my stress, anxiety and lack of sleep, along with the physical demands of dancing so much, might have pushed my body to the point where, given some precipitating factor, such as a virus, it could no longer take the strain. And while I didn't believe that I had created my illness in order to get my father's attention, I knew that my caring and pragmatic cardiologist father would be able to help me now. I called him, explained what was going on and told him that I was coming home.

My dad made an appointment for me with an internist who shared his suite of offices, and I went to see him the day after I arrived. The doctor knew I had just been diagnosed and probably assumed, because of my age and because my blood sugar levels were high, but nowhere near as high as would be expected with uncontrolled type 1 diabetes, that I had adult-onset, or type 2, diabetes. At the time it was not as common as it is now for an adult to be diagnosed with type 1 or for a child to have type 2, which is generally associated with lifestyle—being overweight and inactive. Type 1 diabetes is generally thought of as "childhood" diabetes, which is usually associated with the image of a slender young child giving herself insulin injections. Type 1 diabetes is caused by an antibody—part of the body's immune system that makes a mistake and starts attacking the insulin-producing cells, the beta cells, in the pancreas. This is called an autoimmune process (auto = self and immune = infection-fighting system) and is not reversible. People who develop type 1 diabetes have to take insulin for life. Type 2 diabetes means that the body becomes resistant to the effects of insulin, and the body also stops making enough insulin. Most people who get this type of diabetes are inactive and overweight. The treatment starts with weight loss and exercise, then goes to oral medications and may ultimately require insulin. Almost everyone who gets type 2 diabetes has a family history of diabetes, which is much rarer in type 1 diabetes. Nowadays, we know that people can get either type of diabetes at any age, but a slender, athletic person in their twenties almost certainly has type 1 diabetes and requires insulin injections, not pills, for treatment.

At the time, however, it was generally assumed that a diagnosis of diabetes in an adult indicated type 2. This doctor's treatment of me wasn't very different from that of the one I'd seen in New York. He checked my blood sugar level but did very little else.

He did not, for example, do a test to determine how much, if any, insulin my pancreas was producing. He spent almost no time talking to me, and my brain was so foggy that I didn't have the wherewithal to ask any questions. What he did do was to pre-scribe an oral medication that he said would lower my blood sugar levels. As it turned out, the medication was intended for people with type 2 diabetes to cause their pancreas to increase its insulin production; but in type 1 diabetes it can actually be dangerous because it can exhaust the pancreas entirely. And, finally, he sent me to a nutritionist next door, who was now the third person not to explain what was happening to me or why. Instead of teaching me the intricacies of the effects of food on blood sugar levels, and how I could balance food, activity and blood sugars, she just gave me a general list of foods and their carbohydrate content and told me what I could or couldn't eat.

I understood that the purpose of the list was to accommodate people's cravings, and I knew about cravings. Even though I'd gotten over my Entenmann's doughnut habit, I was still an emo-tional eater and now I was also ravenous because my blood sugars were so high. There were tons of sugar in my bloodstream but it wasn't going into my cells, which needed fuel. So I was rave-nously hungry. I was literally starving and didn't know it. But I didn't want to give into my emotional and physiological impulses. I didn't want to know how to *accommodate* my diabetes. I wanted to know how to cure it.

The doctor had said that I needed to check my blood sugar regularly, so Dad took me to a diabetes center where we bought a home blood glucose monitor. The people at the center explained how I was supposed to use it. These days, blood sugar readings can be completed in a matter of seconds with a lot less blood, but at the time I was diagnosed the process took much longer and was much more complicated. First I was to turn on the battery-operated monitor, then I was supposed to prick my finger with a sharp device that drew a large droplet of blood. I was to then transfer the blood to a small plastic strip and wait sixty seconds before wiping the blood off the strip with a cotton ball. Lastly, I was to insert the strip into the monitor and wait another sixty seconds for the reading. The whole thing took two minutes, and I was supposed to be doing this several times a day. It seemed incredibly daunting, and what concerned me most was that I was so spacey I didn't know how I was ever going to remember all those steps and details on my own.

After seeing the doctor and the nutritionist and going to buy the monitor, Dad dropped me off at my house. He'd made it clear that I was welcome to stay with him if I wanted to. But after my parents divorced, my father returned to his Orthodox Jewish roots and was now living a strictly observant life with Lynn and their baby, Chava. While I appreciated the offer, I knew that staying at his house, with the many conditions and expectations that would entail, wasn't going to work for me considering what a mess I was at that time.

But life at my mother's wasn't exactly restful, either. Since Romy, my mom and I had been living in New York, we'd given

Michele permission to rent our rooms to her college friends. All the rooms were occupied, so my bed was now a pullout sofa in the living room. Living in the equivalent of a dormitory had been fun when Romy and I were home together and hung out with Michele and her friends. But being sick, feeling the way I did, and living without any privacy in the midst of a bunch of strangers wasn't exactly what I needed.

When Dad dropped me off that day, I went to find a sweater in what had been my closet, but Rob, the guy renting my room, had apparently partied too much the night before, and the room smelled as if he had puked in every corner. I wanted my room back. I needed privacy. I needed a place where I could heal in peace.

I wandered into Michele's room, in the back of the house. She was still at school so I lay down on her bed. Michele had a bunk bed with the top and bottom bunks at right angles to each other. I remember how much I envied her when she got it. Now, even though she was in college, the underbelly of the top bunk was still plastered with posters and teen idol cutouts of sexy men and women. The bottom bunk, where Michele slept, was a waterbed. I lay down, and as I undulated back and forth with the waves and stared at those young, healthy bodies, I thought about how I was feeling. I had been running on adrenaline and endorphins and sheer physical activity for months. Now I felt weak and ill, as if my body were a hundred years old. My brain was so foggy and spacey I could barely hold a thought. My stomach burned with hunger and no amount of food could satisfy me. I couldn't stop drinking and I was peeing constantly.

I knew that I'd had these symptoms to some degree or another for a while, but they hadn't been so bad that I couldn't keep dancing, and I had chalked it all up to being tired and stressed. Clearly I'd been denying what my body had been trying to tell me. My excessive urinating was because the sugar in my blood was spilling out through my kidneys and pulling water out with it, dehydrating me all day and all night long. The more I drank the more I peed, and since I couldn't stop the peeing, I couldn't stop the drinking. My body desperately needed to get back into balance, with sugar in my cells, not outside of my cells, so I could once again have strength and energy. Now I wondered if I should try to find that Philippine healer, who seemed to have detected my problem before I was even aware of it. But then it seemed like an impossible task to track him down and maybe have to follow him from city to city, not to mention how much money that would cost.

I needed someone to take me by the hand and guide me. And then it hit me—the perfect person was right there in my own family. Grandma!

TWENTY-TWO

My grandmother Gloria had not only been a professional dancer and choreographer, she was also a health food nut. In fact, she had been an advocate of health food before it had a name. She baked her own wheat bread, grew and ate organic foods, and made her own fresh carrot juice daily.

As a young kid I used to love Grandma's kitchen. There were dozens of jars of nuts and seeds: cashews, pecans, walnuts, as well as sunflower, sesame and pumpkin seeds. There was also a big jar of chewable vitamin C that Grandpa called *chee chees,* and that tasted like candy to me. As far back as I can remember, Grandma had been preparing healthful meals. She served papaya fifteen minutes before the meal to aid our digestion. Then came a salad with raw vegetables like jicama, cilantro, radish, scallion, red leaf lettuce, beets and carrots. Her salads were always a beautiful mélange of brilliant colors. The dressing was homemade, a combination of olive oil, herbs and Bragg amino acids, that was so good she could have bottled and sold it. Then came fish or chicken baked with herbs and spices. We always had herbal tea at the end of the meal. Everything was so good that I had never thought of healthful food as anything less than delicious.

But beyond being a spectacularly healthy cook, Grandma was a fighter. When she believed in something, nothing could stop her. There was the time, for example, when my grandparents were living in Shaker Heights, Ohio, and all the Dutch elms in the city had been infected with a virus. No one could stop the trees from spreading the disease or from dying. The city officials wanted to cut down all the elms in Grandma's front yard, but rather than comply and lose her trees, she brought in a Dutch elm tree expert, who tested the soil and replaced it. Because of her, a whole city of trees was saved.

Grandma was definitely the person I needed. I called her and explained my diagnosis. "I need someone to help me get my body working again," I said. "Could I come and live with you, Grandma?"

"Will you do what I tell you to do?" she asked.

"Yes, Grandma, I promise."

So I packed up, said goodbye to Michele and her friends and went to live with my grandparents.

Grandma and Grandpa lived in Mountain Gate, a gated community high above the 405 freeway overlooking the city and valleys below.

Grandma put me in the guest room on the second floor. It was decorated in soothing light blue tones with a plush carpet and **was bigger than the** living room in my New York apartment. At last, I had peace. It was a relief to be someplace familiar where I could feel safe.

Even before I'd unpacked my bags, Grandma had devised a plan, which was, quite simply, to focus on what I should eat. I was to drink fresh vegetable juices consisting mainly of spinach, cucumber and green beans with a little carrot. I was also to eat lots of raw vegetables, a little fruit, some nuts and seeds, minimal starches and no processed sugars, because they cause blood sugar levels to spike, and no processed foods. Everything was organic: no pesticides, hormones or antibiotics. And since I didn't sleep well, Grandma said no coffee, only herbal tea. No coffee! Since joining the company I had lived on coffee, diet soda and muffins. But I was committed to Grandma's regime even though I was dying for my morning caffeine and carbs and was having a hard time getting out of bed.

I remembered being a little girl and watching with my sisters and brother as Grandma handed Grandpa his pillbox before every meal. It was full of vitamins in every shape and color imaginable. There were pills for his heart, his liver, his kidneys, even his brain. He'd pick them out, one at a time, say what each one was for and then swallow it. We all wanted to take them, too.

Now Grandpa and I were swallowing our vitamins together. We both held our nose as we guzzled down our cod liver oil. He hated it as much as I did, but he wanted me to dance again and knew that if anyone could help me it was Grandma.

Even though he could be hard on me when I was a little girl, Grandpa was one of my most enthusiastic fans. Since I'd joined

City Ballet, he'd made numerous trips to New York to see me perform and spend time with me. While Grandma was the queen of healthy eating, Grandpa was the king of positive thinking. In fact, he turned out to be a real softie. Grandma was the tough one, and now both he and I were doing as we were told.

Grandma and I gathered an enormous pile of books and went through each and every one of them. I finally began to understand exactly what this disease was about. I learned that blood sugar levels affect every one of us, but when you have diabetes, controlling your blood sugar level is a constant concern.

In order for the body to function properly, the cells need to be fed. Cells get their nourishment from the foods we eat, which are broken down in the body and circulate through our bloodstream as "sugar." That "sugar" needs to travel from the bloodstream to the cells, and what makes this happen is a hormone called insulin. When the body senses that there is sugar in the bloodstream, the body releases insulin. In a normal body, insulin is like a key that unlocks a door and lets the sugar into the cells. But a person with diabetes has one of two problems. In type 1 diabetes, the body manufactures little to no insulin. In type 2, the insulin is available but the body doesn't utilize it properly. Either way, the sugar remains in the blood and creates what are called high blood sugar levels. A high blood sugar level is a sign that your cells are being starved. And starved cells can lead to anything from heart disease or stroke to kidney failure, blindness, circulatory problems and amputations.

As I have said, while type 1 *always* requires insulin, the treatment for type 2 diabetes is a diet and exercise regimen, often with oral medication and sometimes also insulin. Since neither of the doctors I'd been to had even suggested my taking insulin, I naturally assumed, as the doctor apparently had, that I had type 2 diabetes, which meant that I could reverse it with medication, diet and exercise. But if that was true, it also meant that I'd somehow brought the disease on myself because of my poor lifestyle choices. I blamed my emotional eating, poor sleep habits and stressful career. I knew I couldn't exercise any more than I had been (in fact, in retrospect, it was probably dancing as much as I did that had kept my blood sugar levels from rising even higher), but I could eat healthier and I could try to do more to control my anxiety.

Three days and forty books later, Grandma and I came to the conclusion that what you ate did make a difference, but the books didn't seem to agree on what that should be. Some said to count carbohydrates, and to eat a lot of them. Some said to avoid carbs altogether. At that point I was more confused than ever, and my monitor was telling me that my blood sugar levels were still out of control. Grandma and I decided that her diet was better than any of them and that we could figure this out on our own.

We analyzed every morsel I ate and how it affected my blood sugar levels. I was using my monitor thirty minutes after each meal, between meals and right before the next.

We noticed that my numbers were high after breakfast and tried to figure out why. Breakfast consisted of two eggs, a piece of toast with butter and half an orange. We guessed it was the fruit sugar in the orange or the carbohydrate in the toast. After a week we started to see a pattern. Red apples elevated my blood sugars higher than green, and beans alone caused them to rise more than beans with chicken. White rice caused more of a spike than brown rice but not as much when combined with a protein or fat like nuts, seeds or olive oil.

My mom and Romy called from New York every day, but I still didn't want to talk to any of my friends from the company. I'd told my grandmother that if any of them called she should tell them I wasn't home. They were all still performing every night, and just thinking about the theater got me so upset that I'd want to cheat on my diet. On the one hand, I was determined to reverse my diabetes, and I had confidence in Grandma's diet. On the other hand, all I could do was cry. I was trying as hard as I could to do whatever it took to get back to New York and dance. But I was afraid I wouldn't make it. My body was tired and my soul was tired from trying to be strong.

I'd been checking my blood at least twenty times a day, and the numbers had been consistently in the high 200s or the low 300s. Normal blood sugar levels range from 70 to 110. Then, at the end of the second week, I was checking as usual when I looked at the monitor and saw a number in the low 200s. Apparently the medication and Grandma's diet were working!

Just to be sure, I pricked my finger again, waited for the beep, and sure enough, the numbers started coming down. Grandma

Riding my beloved pony, Gent, at age 10.

At Sheila Rozann's studio, where I learned to dance, age 13.

I have a long family history of dancing. This is my grandmother, Gloria, as a young dancer.

The Levand Family Dancers. From left to right: my grandmother, my Aunt Arlene and my mother. They performed this act at a hospital in Cleveland for soldiers wounded in World War II.

My mother continued to dance throughout my childhood, while working full-time and raising four kids. Here she is in full costume for one of her folk dance performances.

My mother and grandmother in 1998—still dancing!

As a Snowflake in *The Nutcracker*. This was my first year as a
member of the corps de ballet of NYCB, 1984.
Choreography by George Balanchine © The George Balanchine Trust.

My first leading role, as the Sugarplum Fairy in *The Nutcracker*. This was taken the year before I was diagnosed with diabetes.
Photo © Paul Kolnik. Choreography by George Balanchine © The George Balanchine Trust.

Dancing with Peter Boal in the premier of *Les Petits Riens*.
This was taken days before my diagnosis, when I was very
sick, and had no idea my life was in danger.
© *Steven Caras, 2009, all rights reserved.*
Choreography by Peter Martins.

With Ben Huys in *Four Gnossiennes*. I was dangerously
underweight because I had been misdiagnosed
again and wasn't on insulin.
Photo © Paul Kolnik. Choreography by Peter Martins.

The grand pas de deux with Ben Huys from *The Nutcracker*, which I danced in regularly with NYCB.
Photo © Paul Kolnik. Choreography by George Balanchine
© The George Balanchine Trust.

This photo was taken soon after I retired from NYCB in 2002, and was featured in a calendar of people living successfully with diabetes.
© Sue Bennett Archive 2009.

At a Taking Control of Your Diabetes conference around 2004, where I led a group of people with diabetes in movement exercises.

Today, at home in California, healthier and happier than ever.
Photo by Mark Harmel.

and I were elated. We hugged each other tight. Grandma was beaming. For the first time in weeks, I smiled.

Still, I had a long way to go. Even though my numbers were coming down periodically, they were still too high. I was still dizzy, and I was famished all the time. I wanted to devour every bit of food in the entire kitchen. A pound of almonds or cashew nuts would have been a good start. It wasn't easy to stick to my diet, but with my ever-vigilant grandmother hovering, I did.

About that time, I started to feel that I could handle saying hello to my friends. I missed them and I missed my life, so the next time my friend Jeff called, I told Grandma I'd take the call.

Jeff Edwards was one of my closest male friends. We could talk about anything. He was a gorgeous dancer with a bright future who had been with me in the cast of *Les Petits Riens* and frequently worked out with me at Julio's studio.

"How are you feeling, Zippy?" he asked.

I said I was better and then I asked how he was doing. The season had just finished and the company was now on their three-week layoff.

"Great," he said. "At the end of the season, just when you left…" And he went on to tell me about all the dancers who'd been chosen for all the parts I would have given anything to dance. I wasn't ready to hear it.

After I hung up, I walked slowly back to my room. I wasn't smiling now, and my occasional "better" blood sugar test didn't seem like such a big deal. I wasn't mad at Jeff. He simply assumed that I would be back and as good as new. Since I didn't tell him, he had no idea how much I was still struggling.

When I'd been at my grandmother's for about two weeks, my aunt Rhonda redeemed herself from her comments about my trying to get my father's attention by giving me a list of healers. One in particular drew my interest.

Jenni was a Native American medicine woman who lived about half an hour away. I scheduled an appointment with her. When I got there, she told me to lie down on a massage table, rubbed my body with oils and made a list of herbs I was to prepare and drink three times a day. As I lay there on her table with crystals at my head, she told me that something good would come from all this and that someday I would write a book about what I was experiencing. I decided she was trying to be kind, and I appreciated that, but I thought she must be crazy.

After four weeks on Grandma's diet, taking Jenni's herbs and the oral medication, my blood sugars returned to normal. My head cleared. My moods stabilized and I no longer felt so hopeless. My stomach stopped its constant rumbling. My cravings abated, my thirst was quenched, and I no longer spent the day running to the bathroom. I was elated. Since my assumption, as well as that of the doctors I'd seen, was that I had type 2 diabetes, I quite naturally believed that what I'd been doing had worked—I'd taken control of my disease. It wasn't until later that I found out I was in the "honeymoon stage" of type 1

diabetes, during which time there is some spontaneous restoration of insulin production. Undoubtedly my diet had helped,
but, as I would soon discover, it wasn't a cure.

One of the things I'd learned from reading all those books and
was now experiencing firsthand is that there's a close relationship between unstable blood sugar levels, cravings and emotional
turmoil. When my sugars were out of control, so were my cravings
and moods. Now that my levels had normalized, I was starting to
feel more like my old self. I had more energy and started doing
tendus and pliés while holding on to the bathroom sink. I even
did some *relevés* to reacquaint my feet w ith pointe shoes.

It was just in the nick of time. Rehearsals for the spring season
were about to begin. I had been away from the company for five
weeks. I wasn't sure I was ready to return, but I needed to try. I
had to be in company class. I had to get back there before they
forgot about me.

I needed to move and dance again.

PART FIVE

Dancing with Diabetes

TWENTY-THREE

Back in New York, the company had been off for three weeks and I hadn't danced in five. On the first morning of rehearsals for the spring season, many thoughts ran through my mind. Peter Martins would be teaching company class. Peter's classes were always technical and difficult. Was I crazy to think I'd have the muscle strength and stamina to get through it? Had people been talking about me while I was away? Did everyone know about my illness? Would they be staring at me? Would my blood sugar levels be okay?

I didn't know, but in the end I was more worried about what people would think if I weren't in class—that there was something terribly wrong with me, that I was even sicker than they had thought—than I was about being there and dancing poorly.

The first thing I did when I woke up was to check my blood sugar levels, as I did every morning now. I still found it hard to get the right spot, just at the outer part of the padding of the finger. That morning I saw a big droplet of blood, large enough to fill the entire strip, which is what you needed in those days to get a proper reading. Good, I had hit it right this time. I followed the steps, put the strip into the slot on the front of the meter and waited. I hated this part—waiting for the result, the moment of judgment that would tell me whether or not my levels were okay.

My fingers looked like a pincushion from being pricked all day. As of last week my readings were still above 200 at times. Beep, the meter made its annoying sound: 118. Great, my blood sugar levels were within the high normal range.

I decided to eat a couple of eggs, organic of course, with no cereal or toast. The eggs were solid protein and wouldn't raise my sugars. I couldn't afford to be spaced out today. I got dressed, packed my leotards, tights and pointe shoes in my dance bag, and headed out the door. Romy and I were now living on West End Avenue and Seventy-fourth Street, in the part-residential Esplanade Hotel.

On my way to the elevator, I was comforted by the familiar laughter of the youthful African cast of the Broadway hit *Sarafina!* Their voices reverberated throughout the floor as they sang and danced to rhythms that made me wish I could shake my body and move so freely. I was feeling pretty stiff and preoccupied with how I might not be able to stand perfectly on one foot in Peter's class. As I passed their rooms, I tried to let their songs and earthy freedom loosen me up.

I briskly walked the twelve blocks to the theater. I could do the half mile in twelve minutes if I didn't have to wait at a stoplight. That was more exercise than I'd had in more than a month. It felt so great to be outside and moving again. Spring had arrived in New York and the air from the Hudson River was crisp and clean. On my way, I passed the fruit and vegetable market on the corner of Seventy-second Street. It had a great salad bar where I used to pick up dinner after the performance. I loved the tuna salad, the rice and bean mix, and the vegetables in some exotic sauce. How would my sugars react to those foods now?

There was Luv's, the drug store where I bought my false eye-lashes, eyelash glue, and the baby oil and cotton balls I used to remove my stage makeup. The best part of the walk was the iconic fountain at Lincoln Center. Today, a light breeze blew a spray of water that covered me with a gentle mist. I felt like I was home.

I went through the back stage door and down the stairs where I greeted the guard, who always said, "Hello, Zippora," as I entered each day—the same one who had kept pointing to the message board reminding me of the notice from my doctor that I continually ignored.

Inside the theater, I took the elevator to the fourth-floor dressing rooms for corps de ballet ladies. I changed into my leotard and tights, covered myself in sweats, and went up to the fifth-floor rehearsal hall. As I made my way along the cement hallway, I began to shake. What was happening? I felt as if I might pass out at any second.

I ran back to the dressing room, now starting to fill up with dancers chatting about their vacations and complaining about how fat and out of shape they were. I was moving fast; no one seemed to notice me. I took my meter into the bathroom. I was shaking so much that the prick wasn't easy. Forty-five, forty-six, the meter counted. I was afraid that another dancer might hear the loud beep of the meter, so I flushed the toilet to drown out the embarrassing sound. Two minutes later my number was displayed—52, way too low. I was having my first low blood sugar attack.

Even though I hadn't yet experienced what low blood sugar was like, I'd been told numerous times about how it would feel. The shaking—which felt like a minor earthquake inside my body—was one of the key symptoms I'd been warned about.

I needed something sweet and I needed it fast. I didn't know at that point that I ought to be carrying something sweet with me at all times. I ran to the vending machine, shoved in my change and guzzled down a can of orange juice.

A few minutes later I walked into the rehearsal hall determined not to let anyone see that I was still mildly shaking. In a few minutes, the juice would hit my bloodstream and I'd be fine.

The room was full of formerly pale dancers, now tanned from island vacations and greeting one another with hugs and kisses. Stacey and Catherine came running up to give me big hugs. Other dancers asked if I was okay. Suzanne Farrell, Patricia McBride and Heather Watts each gave me a nod to show their support.

"Everything is great, I'm fine," I repeated over and over with a thank-you-for-caring smile. But was I really okay, or was this just my best performance yet? Still shaking, I slid into a split and stretched my legs. Suddenly, the loud buzz in the room abruptly ceased. I turned, and sure enough, the silence meant that Peter Martins had entered the studio. The shaking had stopped, so the orange juice had worked to restore my blood sugar just in the nick of time.

The pianist started playing softly. With no direction we stood at the barre, took first position and began bending our knees in a plié. It felt so good to move up and down to the rhythm of the music. Most of all, it was good to be back in the community of dancers and feeling that I belonged.

As we began our *tendus,* Peter circled the room, giving corrections to one dancer after another. Then, suddenly, he walked in my direction. As he came closer, my heart began beating so fast that I felt as if it were going to pound right out of my chest. This was not a diabetic symptom. It was nerves.

Peter grabbed my hand. I took a deep breath, and I lifted my head and chest as if I were in the army and my commander had singled me out for an order. Still pointing my toes as hard as I could, I gathered up my courage and glanced at Peter out of the corner of my eye.

"Are you all better now?" he asked.

"Yes, Peter, I'm all better now."

He smiled, nodded and walked away. Was that it? Was that all I had to say? As if I had caught a cold and now it was gone? Maybe it *was* gone.

The doctor had said, and everything I read had confirmed, that exercise would bring down blood sugar levels, and help the medication work better. If my low blood sugar attack was the result of my no-carb breakfast and a brisk ten-minute walk to the theater, maybe, now that I'd be exercising all day, I could cut down on the oral medication the doctor had prescribed. Maybe someday I wouldn't need medication at all. At least that's what I hoped.

TWENTY-FOUR

After the first week, all-day rehearsals resumed. I was so physically sore from Peter's classes and from rehearsing six hours a day that I couldn't walk without pain. Every toe had a blister, but I didn't care. I was just ecstatic to be there and to realize that no one seemed to care about my diagnosis. Now all I needed to figure out was how to keep my blood sugars normal.

Whether it was because I was still in the honeymoon stage of my illness or because my body was still producing a small amount of insulin, the constant exercise and strict Grandma diet combined with the medication continued to bring my sugars down. Too much, in fact. I constantly felt shaky and tried to hide it. I kept a supply of quick-acting sugar like dried figs in my dance bag, and whenever Rosemary stopped the music to correct another dancer, I quickly popped a fig in my mouth, hoping that no one could see what I was doing.

When I called my doctor in L.A. and told him that I was having continual low blood sugars, he told me to cut back on the medication. Following his instructions, I continued to reduce the dose until eventually I stopped taking it altogether. Elated, I was now completely convinced that I had "overcome" my disease with a healthy diet, exercise and determination. I vowed to only eat foods that wouldn't raise my blood sugar levels and to dance all day long.

Now that I was more confident, I was able to reconsider Rhonda's suggestion that, on some level, I had created my situation. I began to read spiritual books about why people become ill as well as stories about those who had succeeded in overcoming their illnesses. I needed to understand why some people got sick, and I wanted to know how other people felt about what had happened to them.

One of the books was written by a blind man who had regained his sight by using visualization techniques. He taught specific exercises, things to think and times to practice. I had been a believer ever since Suzanne Farrell taught me to use visualization before my debut as Sugar Plum. Now I started visualizing my pancreas healed and in perfect working order.

I was a disciplined dancer with a plan: A plus B equals C. I figured that as long as I was rigid about my routine, I wouldn't have to go back on medication. Sometimes, though, it wasn't so easy. Disciplined as I wanted to be, perfect as I expected I should be (especially since I was now aware of the consequences of not being perfect), sometimes I just couldn't resist that extra bite—or two or three—of an apple or pear. I simply had to eat the whole thing, even though I knew my sugars were going to be high the next time I checked them. I'd try to talk myself out of it, but I'd take those bites, anyway, and then the guilt and self-blame would kick in. I wondered what was wrong and why I couldn't control myself.

In the end, however, self-discipline prevailed. Sure, I had slipups, but I'd get back on track pretty quickly—I had to because the repercussions of doing otherwise were unacceptable—and by the next day my levels would go down again. Every time I ate I'd test myself with the meter. I was becoming more and more obsessive about my food, exercise and blood sugar levels. But it was worth it because my plan was working. To me, the situation was a challenge, and for a full year and a half after I returned to the company in the spring of 1987, I managed to turn it into a major success story. I may have been obsessive about diet, exercise and blood sugar levels, but it was worth it because I was dancing and living without insulin or medication.

I felt as if I had everything under control. Every potential problem seemed to have an easy solution. So when, in the early fall of 1988, the company set off on a two-week tour of Japan, I packed almonds and cans of tuna fish, just in case I needed a quick, low-carb snack.

This was my first international tour, and Romy's very first tour with the company. There were a lot of new dancers now, all of us chosen by Peter, so I felt insulated by my close friends as well as by my sister and her friends.

Romy and I strolled through the airport, and I remember seeing Patricia McBride buying a scarf, Suzanne Farrell reading her book in the café, a group of older corps dancers smoking in the restaurants. They were all so cool; so chic. It had never occurred to me to get dressed up for a night flight, so I was wearing comfortable pants and feeling drab and ordinary. Still, traveling as a member of the New York City Ballet, I couldn't help feeling a part of the glamour in some way.

On the plane I sat next to Romy, and for the most part, we were quiet. She wanted to know how I was coping. I wanted to know how she was doing, but neither of us offered much information. Romy was in a relationship with a dancer in the company, and I suspected things were not going well—otherwise, why would she be sitting with me instead of him? But she didn't confide in me, so I couldn't be sure. We were in a bit of an awkward phase, Romy being in her first relationship, confiding in her friends more than me, and me obsessing about my health and dancing. We were experiencing different worlds. But it was still nice to have her by my side.

Romy dozed, and I tried to sleep, too, but I couldn't. I stayed awake the entire flight and, consequently, arrived in Japan exhausted. We had one day off before rehearsals and performances began, so there wasn't very much time to adjust to the vastly different time zone. After rehearsing all day and performing at night, I couldn't wait to get some sleep, but when I finally did go to bed, I would lie there totally awake, like the old days when I couldn't wind down after performances. My sugars were okay, but something else was obviously completely off. My body could not adjust, and I couldn't fall asleep.

I didn't want anyone to know I was having a problem, because I didn't want anyone to suspect that it might have something to do with my diabetes. I rehearsed by day and performed each night with all the energy and enthusiasm I could muster. But night after night, I didn't sleep. I was so upset about having a problem no one else seemed to be having that I didn't even tell the physical therapist. And I didn't tell Romy, either. She was having fun and I didn't want to bother her with something she couldn't have fixed in any case.

Being on tour far from home was a license for company members to let go. After dancing all day and night, different groups hung out together, secret liaisons were made, and friends got a chance to spend some time together. Touring was fun and glamorous—but not for me, at least this time.

I was dazed and dizzy from sleep deprivation. I didn't care that my sister and my friends were out living it up while I was alone in my hotel room eating my almonds and tuna fish and checking my blood sugars. All I wanted to do was to sleep. We performed in Japan for two weeks and I slept for a total of about two hours.

A lot of dancers had made plans to stay in the Far East once the tour ended. Romy and I went with a group to Thailand. It had been almost twenty years since we'd lived there, and I looked forward to returning as a dancer with the New York City Ballet to the place where my life as a dancer began.

I wanted to relax and enjoy it, but I was nearly delirious by the time we got there. In Japan, my sugars had stayed normal from dancing all day and performing every night, but once the performing and exercising ended, my levels shot up so high that I couldn't lower them no matter how well I ate. With my sugars soaring and no medication in my bag, I began to panic. Had I been living in some kind of fantasy world thinking that I'd conquered my diabetes? I could no longer avoid the truth: eating perfectly and dancing all day was not enough to keep my diabetes in control. I was supposed to stay in Thailand another week, but I changed my ticket and flew back to New York.

TWENTY-FIVE

I needed to find a good doctor, one whom I could trust, in the city. Since I'd stopped taking my medication, I hadn't been in touch with the doctor in L.A., and there was no way I was going back to the woman who had diagnosed me. I was still angry with her for having broken confidentiality and telling another dancer about my diagnosis.

I had read a book by a well-known and highly respected diabetes specialist whose protocol I really liked. His approach to diabetes called for avoiding complications by adhering to a strict blood-sugar-monitoring regime and a rigid diet plan. He was a pioneer, adamant that blood sugars be kept as close to normal as possible. At that time most doctors preferred to allow their patients' levels to be a little high rather than put them at increased risk for low blood sugars, which could lead to insulin shock and death. But recent studies had shown that good blood sugar control was the key to avoiding the terrible consequences of high blood sugar levels, which had terrified me ever since I was diagnosed. This doctor, who was himself a type 1 diabetic, had been saying for years what was now being proved.

I knew the discipline wouldn't be a problem for me because I had been successful for so long controlling my sugars with only minor slipups. I'd follow any regime, no matter how strict, if it meant keeping my limbs, and staying on my toes.

I first saw my new doctor on a cold fall day, reluctant to admit that I needed to keep this appointment, but forcing myself to follow through and end my denial.

The doctor looked over my previous blood work and listened to my story. He was personable and thorough and took a lot of time with me. I had not had this sort of treatment from a doctor before, and I liked him.

Then he offered his diagnosis: I had type 1, or insulin-dependent, diabetes.

I was stunned. Why hadn't either of my previous doctors discovered it? This guy had to be mistaken.

He went on to explain that, for reasons unknown, my immune system was attacking itself and had burned out the insulin-producing cells of my pancreas. "You're lucky," he said. "Most likely you're still putting out a tiny bit of your own insulin. That's why the medication worked and why it sent you into low blood sugars."

But the medication was ultimately having the destructive effect of pushing the islet cells of my pancreas to burn out faster. In time, it could burn out completely. There was no home remedy—

be it Grandma's diet, visualization, exercising all day or packing healthy snacks—that could even begin to restore the damaged cells. All my attempts to heal myself had been useless; in fact, the medication I'd been taking may have put me at further risk.

As the doctor continued talking, his tone was compassionate. He's the one who explained to me the honeymoon period, when for up to two years after the onset of type 1 diabetes there can be some spontaneous restoration of insulin production. But, he warned, "It's only a temporary situation, not an indication that the diabetes is improving, or in remission or cured. The exercise and your diet saved you—for a time."

I wondered if the lack of sleep in Japan had pushed my system over the edge, but I didn't bother asking. What was the use? The honeymoon was over.

Then he spoke the words I never wanted to hear: "You will have to take insulin injections for the rest of your life."

I got a huge lump in my throat and I wanted to cry, but I wouldn't let myself. Not there, not then. I stared blankly ahead as he went on to explain the other requirements of his protocol.

I'd have to check my blood sugar levels at least ten times a day to achieve the tight control he hoped for, which I'd been doing, anyway. And he strongly recommended a no-carbohydrate diet, which would also be easy for me. In fact, I wouldn't have to alter my diet at all, because Grandma's low-to-no-carbohydrate diet was really just a more healthful version of his.

When he'd finished his explanation, it was time to learn how to give myself the shot. I followed the doctor into another room, where he checked my blood sugar level. It was at 200. He then calculated how much insulin I would need to bring it into the normal range of 70 to 120, his ideal target range.

The doctor took out a syringe and showed me the little lines indicating the number of units of insulin. Then he stuck the needle into the insulin vial, pushed the plunger forward and filled the vial with two units of air. Very slowly, with the needle still in the vial, he pulled the plunger back, letting the insulin fill the syringe. Then he flicked it with his finger to get the bubbles out. He made it look easy, but I wasn't convinced it really was. Today I use a prefilled insulin pen, which is a much easier delivery system that uses a thinner, less painful needle. But at the time there were no insulin pens.

He showed me all the areas where I could shoot: the fatty part of my upper arm, my stomach, my butt and my legs. He turned toward me with the needle in his hand and the insulin intact. As he asked me to pull up my sleeve, this sweet doctor with the constant grin began to look to me like Dr. Frankenstein. Then wham! He jabbed my upper arm. It was the tiniest pinch. I didn't like it, but it wasn't so bad.

Still, my head was spinning.

It was a lot to deal with. There was a different kind of insulin to inject at night, one that lasted longer. The stomach and buttocks were better for that. I'd have to check my levels and then figure out how much insulin to take. This was scary. The tiniest bit too much and I could go too low.

"Exercise acts like insulin," the doctor said. "So if you're working out, be careful. It can be very dangerous."

From everything I'd been reading, I knew about the risk of taking too much insulin, the worst-case scenario being insulin shock and even potential death.

I couldn't even think about that possibility, so I focused on smaller things. The thought of sticking a needle into my skin wasn't pleasant, but I was more alarmed about how I was going to juggle everything I needed to do and remember to do it. Yes, exercise was crucial and beneficial, but I wondered if my doctor realized how *much* I exercised. He knew I was a professional dancer, and I tried to explain that I danced up to seven-and-a-half hours in class and rehearsals and an additional three hours in a full-out performance. I wasn't sure that I was making myself clear. Not many people realize that being a ballerina is one of the most athletic careers you can have.

As I left the doctor's office, it all started to hit me. I looked at the needles and syringes he'd given me. Rehearsing all day and performing every night, how on earth would I know how much insulin to take? The protocol he had put me on required that I take a shot any time my blood sugars were even a tiny bit above normal. Keeping one's levels within normal range is certainly the ideal. But I would have to carefully calculate the correct dose, taking my level of exercise into consideration. How would I figure out how much I needed without overdoing it? It would be like walking a tightrope. It seemed nearly impossible.

TWENTY-SIX

My thoughts were racing off in every direction. On the one hand, nothing was going to take my career away from me. I had to dance. And I had to admit to myself that more than anything I hoped to someday be a soloist ballerina. Performing was the greatest joy of my life. It *was* my life. Nothing would stop me.

On the other hand, I felt defeated. Suddenly my dreams seemed entirely out of reach. I feared that I wouldn't be able to do the things I dreamed of doing. I thought about Jerry Robbins's not having chosen me to repeat my role in *The Goldberg Variations* or for any other lead in almost two years. I remembered how he had walked away during my solo in *Les Petits Riens.* Jerry hated weakness in any form. To my mind, it now seemed that he must have sensed what was going on in my body. Of course, in reality, he could have walked away for any number of reasons, but I was convinced that he had left the wing because he didn't want to continue watching me dance. How could I blame him for rejecting me? I would have rejected myself.

Why did I think I could beat the odds? I had wanted a magical, artistic life. What I'd gotten was a new diagnosis. Now my entire world seemed to be crashing down around me.

"Stop being so dramatic!" the voice in my head yelled back at me. "Stop being such a victim. Stop feeling so sorry for yourself. You're young, you dance with the New York City Ballet. You'll find a way even if you won't be Suzanne Farrell. Even if you never get to be a soloist, you'll find a way to manage. You have to dance."

Throughout that winter season and through the spring, I was learning how to dance all day while secretly taking my insulin shots.

Routine is crucial to determining how much insulin to inject. I had no routine. Every ballet was different; some had a lot of jumps and aerobic running around the stage, while others were slow and controlled with little huffing and puffing. Every program was different, as well: some nights I danced in the first ballet; sometimes I danced in all three. I ate lunch at a different time every day. Many days I had so many rehearsals that Rosemary asked me to skip my lunch break altogether.

This meant that the only routine I had was checking my sugars every chance I got. As soon as Rosemary said, "Dancers, take five," I ran to the bathroom and checked my blood. If I was too high I took a shot, too low I ate some figs or dates. I was walking a tightrope, trying to mimic the body's miraculous innate calculations. I had to keep my sugars as close to normal as I could without overdoing it, but it was difficult to gauge exactly how much insulin to take. More often than not, I would take too much and have to eat something sweet to offset it.

Obsessed with my blood sugar numbers, I stopped going to dinner with Catherine and Stacey so I could stay home, eat my own no-carbohydrate food and monitor myself. I was in a different universe from everyone around me. It was not lost on me that as a dancer I was always trying to achieve perfect balance, and now I was trying to perfectly balance my blood sugar levels, as well.

My way of coping was to not let myself give in to my fears, and when I had weak moments I was determined not to let anyone see my struggle. I didn't want to talk about it, not even with Romy or my mother. Now that I was on insulin, I'd given up on the idea that I could heal myself. I just wanted to deal with it, and the only one who could help me with that was my doctor.

I was becoming increasingly isolated, but that's the way I wanted it. One afternoon when everyone else headed out to the deli on our lunch break, I was suddenly hit with a wave of exhaustion. I'd been holding it all together, but in that moment, for some reason, the stress of juggling my blood sugars and trying to keep up with everyone else just felt like too much.

I went to one of the empty dressing rooms, lay down on a cot to nap, and before I knew it, I was crying. I tried not to make any noise in case there was anyone around, so I just lay down on my side, hid my face in the pillow and wept. The next thing I knew there was a dancer lying on the cot beside me, rubbing my back and comforting me. Normally, I would have stopped and pretended to have been asleep, but her soothing hand only made me cry more. While I sobbed quietly, I wondered who it might be. I dreaded turning around and facing this person who was so tender and nurturing in my moment of weakness. Finally, when the tears stopped, I turned around to thank her. There in the cot by my side was my little sister, Romy. Neither of us said a word, but I knew in that moment—if I hadn't before—just how much she loved me.

Having any kind of serious illness is always an isolating experience, and all the more so when everyone around you is so physically strong. For that reason alone, it was particularly meaningful for me to know that I could confide in Romy. My mother was there for me, too. Silent as always, but ever present. It was profoundly comforting to know that they were so unconditionally supportive no matter how distant or uncommunicative I might be.

Slowly, I began to figure out how much exercise each rehearsal and performance required, how it affected my sugar levels, and how much insulin to take. Although I'd given up on Jerry's choosing me for a lead, I never stopped wishing Peter would think of me for something special.

During rehearsal period, the most reliable way to get your schedule was to call a special number and listen to the taped recording of which rehearsals were scheduled for the next day. Calling that number meant that I had to listen to the rehearsal schedule for everyone in the company. Hearing who was learning what roles made me nervous, especially now that I was so afraid of being passed over. I wanted to be happy for the good fortune of others, but I had to admit that it was depressing to hear which younger dancers were learning the roles I longed for.

Then, in the early fall, something fantastic happened. Listening to the recording one evening, I heard my name read out with a long list of principal ladies. Peter Martins had called me to learn one of the five leading ballerina roles in Balanchine's *Divertimento No. 15*, set to music by Mozart.

For a while after *Les Petits Riens,* which I had come to associate with my diabetes diagnosis, I couldn't even listen to Mozart's music. I'd even grown to hate yellow, the color of my costume. But that was now all in the past. *Divert* was the perfect ballet for me. It's a classical "tutu" ballet. It isn't one of the hardest of his ballets, and although it requires strength, it's all about purity of movement, heart and soul. It's the kind of ballet I love the most— classical with Balanchine's signature modern touches.

This was the third big role for which Peter had chosen me. It meant that he still wanted to use me, even after my diagnosis.

The company would be leaving for a European tour before the beginning of the fall season in New York, and *Divert* was to be one of the pieces we'd perform on that tour. We rehearsed for a couple of weeks before Peter came to watch the various casts. He had to decide who would dance with whom and on which night. When casting was posted the week before we left for Europe, my name was listed with the first cast. I was the only one among the five ladies dancing leads who was still in the corps de ballet. I was elated. This was such a boost of confidence for me.

Over the next days, I went out with Catherine, visited Stacey and hung out with my mom and Romy. I felt alive again. The smile I had faked for so many months finally felt real. I was elated to know that Peter still wanted to use me and to once again experience the artistic freedom I got from dancing a leading role.

TWENTY-SEVEN

In the early fall, the company set off for Europe for the first time since Balanchine's death. The tour was to start in Copenhagen, Denmark, Peter Martins's birthplace, where we would perform in the theater in Tivoli Gardens, the famous amusement park. It was an extremely important tour for the company, and in particular for Peter.

For me, it was not only my first trip to Europe but also the first time I would be performing a lead while taking insulin. Performing was different from taking class or rehearsing every day, because I wouldn't have the option to stop and check my blood sugars while I was onstage. *Divertimento* was the very first piece on the program opening night. I had no idea how it would go, and I felt a tremendous pressure to show Peter that he hadn't made a mistake by casting me. No one but Romy had any idea what I was up against.

On opening night, I was nervous and excited as I went through my usual preperformance transformation: applying my stage makeup, tightening my hair in a bun, pinning on my rhinestone headpiece. I picked out my pointe shoes, warmed up my body for twenty minutes, then put on my costume. I checked my blood sugar levels: 120. Perfect.

The stage manager called, "Ten minutes, please," and I headed for the stage along with the other dancers in the piece. I thought about Peter Martins watching. I thought about the Queen of Denmark being in the audience.

In the past, even since my diagnosis, the moment right before the curtain rose was when calmness came over me. Once the performance began I was always able to let go and rely on all the work I'd done to prepare. It was the moment I longed to experience, it was what I loved; the moment of the performance where the music took over, the moment when I stopped thinking and my body and the music became one.

As I took my opening position onstage, that didn't happen. Instead, my mind and body tensed. I suddenly worried about my sugars. What if I took too much insulin? What if performing sends them too low? What then?

I tried to calm down by telling myself that I could do it, and that everything would be fine.

The curtain rose and a cool breeze swept the stage.

The first step wasn't so bad as I jumped with one leg bent to the front. Then it all started to go downhill. I almost fell off pointe on the second step, an easy one, with my leg in arabesque. What was going on? This never happened in rehearsals. What were my sugars? Were they off or was this nervousness? As I continued to dance, the only way to combat my nerves was to keep myself completely in the moment. I told myself: Point your toes, extend your arms, hold in your stomach, lift your chest. Oops, I thought, as I stumbled on the next balance. Don't do that again. Here comes another one. Point your toes harder, feel the back foot just as much as the front. More energy, more focus. Damn it, you almost fell over again.

Suddenly my feet went cold. Don't let that stop you, I told myself. Try harder, point harder. My words were like an inner scream. But the louder I screamed at my body, the less it heard me. I was more tired than usual and my legs felt shaky; my head was full and spacey, as if I were under water. By the end of the opening section of the ballet, I had fallen off most of my balances.

Now it was time for my solo. This was what really mattered. "Listen to the music," I told myself. "Try to let go. Think how lovely it is."

When it was time to jump, I barely left the floor.

"It's not working," I screamed silently. "I can't let go."

To let go, I had to stop thinking. But my thoughts never quieted. I prayed for the dance to end.

Finally, the curtain descended. Peter and Rosemary approached the stage to give us corrections. Rosemary went to the corps. From where I stood at the back of the stage with the other four women dancing leads, I saw Peter's shadow in the wing. He had taken a big chance letting me dance a solo on opening night in his hometown. I couldn't look at him. I couldn't handle his disappointment.

Pretending that I hadn't seen him, I quickly turned and ran offstage in the opposite direction.

I raced upstairs to the dressing room, grabbed my meter and hurried into a bathroom stall. My blood sugar level was 150, which wasn't really that high. But it was high enough, combined with my nervousness, to affect my ability to perform well, and according to my doctor's protocol, anything above the normal range was considered too high. I had thought that the exercise would bring down my sugars. It would be a little while before I learned that anxiety and adrenaline can raise them. I had always loved being onstage no matter what role I was dancing. But tonight I had danced poorly, had no fun and I was terrified of what Peter thought.

I hated my body for ruining my life. In the dressing room, I grabbed a syringe, hid it in my sweatshirt and headed to the bathroom, where I jabbed the insulin into my belly.

Another thing I didn't yet know was that exercise has a continuous effect. The dancing I did in *Divert* would probably continue to lower my sugars for hours after the performance was over. I shouldn't have taken a shot of insulin at that moment.

There were two more ballets on the program. I wasn't in the middle piece, but I was in the corps of the last, *Glass Pieces*, one of Jerome Robbins's great works to music by Philip Glass. Jerry was so particular about corps performances that I was as nervous as I would have been dancing a lead. Jerry had rehearsed us every day for weeks before we left on tour, scrutinizing our every movement.

Over the loudspeaker, I heard the stage manager call, "Ten minutes." I put on my costume, a red leotard and black skirt. For this ballet, each dancer wore a particular color leotard and a particular color skirt. Jerry was adamant about which girl should wear what. Sometimes girls tried to switch colors, but Jerry always caught them. He remembered every detail of his ballets. Being impeccable about details was part of what made him great.

Just as "five minutes" was called I began to shake. I was terrified. I worried that I'd taken too much. Before any more thoughts could race through my mind, everything went blank. I'd had low blood sugars before, but something was different this time. Panic surged through my body. Was I going to pass out? Right then? Yes, I felt I was going to black out. "If I don't do something fast, I'm going to lose my mind," I thought. The possibility of insulin shock suddenly flashed in my head.

I bolted back up the stairs to the dressing room and pulled my monitor out of my bag. My hand shook so hard I could barely get the drop of blood I needed onto my strip and into the monitor for the reading. The main roller coaster from Tivoli Gardens happened to go right by the dressing room window. There I was, in the middle of an amusement park, listening to the blissful screams of people on a roller coaster, while I was on a private roller coaster of my own. I threw a handful of glucose tablets down my throat and waited the necessary two minutes for the monitor to do its job. I should have taken them even before I used the monitor, but I wasn't thinking clearly. I knew I was having a severe low blood sugar reaction, but when the monitor finally beeped, I couldn't believe the reading it displayed. Twenty! I didn't know I could still be conscious with my blood sugar that low.

I had never taken glucose tablets before. Although I always had them on hand in case of emergency, I'd never had to take them. Figs and dates had always been enough to give my sugars the boost they needed. How many tablets would I need? I had no idea, so I downed as many as I could. The call "Onstage" came over the loudspeaker.

I ran down the stairs to stage level. *I have to find Romy…where is Romy?* I was in a daze as dancers ran past me toward the stage. I was in all three sections of *Glass Pieces*. As a new member of the company, Romy was just in the second section, in what was essentially a nondancing role. When I found her, she took one look at me and realized that something was terribly wrong. "What's happening to you?" she asked. I couldn't speak.

Romy took charge, pulled me into the changing area and demanded that I take off my costume so that she could put it on and dance my part for me. I could barely think straight, so I took it off and watched as she hurriedly put it on. I put on her orange leotard and black overwrap just as the stage manager called, "Zippora Karz, we are waiting to begin."

"Okay," Romy said, trembling, "tell me what to do."

For a moment we just stared at each other. There were so

many things she would need to know: all my counts and steps, the entrances and exits, coordinating with the other dancers— how could I tell her all this in less than sixty seconds? And the counts for *Glass Pieces* were not the standard two-four or six-eight. It was minimalist music. The counts were two in this direction and five in that, seven over here and ten over there.

There was no way.

"Zippora" again came over the loudspeaker. I said to Romy, "Give me back my costume."

I knew the glucose eventually had to work. Luckily, there was no actual dancing for me in the first two sections, just a lot of patterns and those complicated counts. I don't remember much about the first movement. What I remember most is the second. I was the leader of the line of women who emerge from the wings in silhouette upstage. The whole audience is focused on us. I didn't know if I would remember my counts. But, even more, would the glucose have worked by then or would I pass out? I couldn't faint onstage. I knew it had to work and that I just had to stay in the moment.

"My name is Zippora," I said to myself, trying to keep myself focused, "and I'm going to be all right…one-two-three-four… My name is Zippora, and I'm going to be all right." I talked myself through it and no one seemed to notice. After the performance I went back to the hotel, more concerned that I'd danced poorly than about the health risk I'd created for myself.

Beyond giving me the usual corrections, neither Peter nor

anyone else ever said anything about my performance in *Divert*. I did dance it once more later in the tour, and even though I would, as always, have liked to be better, without the anxieties of opening night my performance was greatly improved.

After Copenhagen, we went on to the Netherlands and Scotland, and then to Paris.

In Paris, after the gala performance, we all dressed in gowns and heels and attended a black tie dinner at the Hôtel de Ville (City Hall). When we arrived, the principals and soloists were escorted to their tables. The corps de ballet dancers were taken to a separate room where there were no tables. Catherine and I were at the buffet, marveling at the architecture and totally oblivious to the fact that there were no soloists or principal dancers in the room, when suddenly principal dancer Ib Andersen came up behind us, sputtering "This is an outrage! Mr. B would never let this happen!"

Ib had been on tour many times with Balanchine, so he knew that ever since the 1934 party for *Serenade,* the first ballet Mr. B had choreographed in America, he always ate with his dancers, including those in the corps de ballet. After that premiere, the audience was served a meal at the Warburg Estate, where *Serenade* had been danced. Balanchine was discovered eating outside with his dancers, who had not been invited in.

"I'm not going to sit in that room with the other principals unless everybody's welcome there," Ib said now. "I'm staying here with you."

Catherine and I blushed and giggled like schoolgirls as he went to get a plate of food.

Like Peter Martins, Ib was Danish and had come to the United States to dance for Balanchine. If Peter Martins was the aristocratic, handsome king, Ib was the angelic boyish prince.

Catherine and I both had a secret crush on him even though he was openly gay. His sexual preference didn't stop women from swooning over him, nor him from flirting with his partners and all the girls. We were amazed that he was talking to us when he could have been with all the "important" people. We thought he was adorable and dreamy. When he returned with his food, we tried to act as if we were really sophisticated.

Back in the hotel room I got into my pajamas and went to brush my teeth. The toothpaste was next to my blood sugar meter, and as I reached for it I knocked the meter so hard that it went crashing to the floor. I picked it up, turned it on and nothing happened. My meter was broken, and it hadn't occurred to me to bring a backup. Until that moment, I hadn't realized that my life was dependent on that monitor. I didn't even own a second one.

I needed to know my blood sugar levels. How much insulin should I take before going to bed? Every night had been different. What should I do? Romy was staying in a different hotel. When I called her in a panic, she told me to call the company's physical therapist.

The therapist traveling with us was named Katy. When I reached her, she tried to calm me down, but I burst into tears.

After hours of trying to phone the States to get a meter sent over-
night, we gave up. It was a weekend, and nothing was going to
happen until Monday.

After I'd spent a sleepless night, Katy took me to a pharmacy
where I paid an exorbitant amount for a meter with a different
calibration system. Reading it was like trying to read Japanese.
Not having that lifeline was terrifying. I sat in the therapy room
sobbing. For months I had tried so hard to hide what was going
on, but now I couldn't hide it any longer. I knew that word of all
this would get back to Peter. What would he think of my consistency and reliability now? I wanted to control my sobbing, but I
couldn't. It was a terrible end to a difficult tour.

TWENTY-EIGHT

I never had another low blood sugar episode as extreme as the one in Copenhagen. Yet I did have them, since I still hadn't learned precisely how much insulin I needed at any given moment and sometimes took too much.

During some performances, I'd shake. When that happened, I'd hope that my sugars weren't dropping so precipitously that I wouldn't be able to maintain my form and dance well. The moment I had an exit from the stage, I'd dash to my dance bag and swallow a handful of glucose tablets, hoping that no one would notice. If anyone did notice, I never knew it.

It was a trying time for me, and the nights were particularly scary. What if I overdid my shot and didn't wake up? By now Romy had moved into her own apartment and my mother was sharing my apartment while I looked for a smaller, more affordable place of my own. Although we had completely separate lives and didn't see each other during the day, I couldn't have had a better, more supportive roommate than my mom. Just knowing that she was there at night was a great comfort.

* * *

For a year and a half—from the fall of 1988 until the spring of 1990—I continued on my rigorous insulin regime. But the constant blood sugar fluctuations were affecting my mood and my dancing. I was trying to get stronger, but it took a while to recover from each low blood sugar episode, and that was taking a toll on me both physically and psychologically. I was trying to prove to myself and to the company that nothing had changed. But I was looking progressively weaker. As much as I liked my doctor and appreciated the value of his protocol—I came to believe that I needed a different approach.

Looking back, I should have handled the situation differently. Had I been more communicative, I could have told the doctor I was having too many low blood sugars. I could have asked him if there was any way we could adjust my insulin dose, and he most likely would have found a way to work that out. But, at the time, it seemed easier to start over with a new doctor than to tell this doctor it wasn't working. As nice as he was, the prospect of confrontation made me nervous and uncomfortable. Instead, I took the coward's way out. I just never went back to him and started all over with someone new. After all that he'd done for me, I regret that I didn't have the tools to explain why his program wasn't working for me.

My new doctor wasn't a diabetes specialist, and couldn't have been more different in his approach. He didn't believe in aggressive insulin therapy to avoid complications. Instead, he leaned toward "looser" control, letting the blood sugars run higher rather than risking the danger of constant lows, which was the therapeutic norm at the time.

When I told him I was taking insulin shots for levels that were just above normal and that I was injecting myself during performances, he gave me a look that said, "That's just ridiculous!"

"It's crazy to play with your health that way," he muttered.

When I told him about my no-carbohydrate diet, he said I should start eating more normally.

"Your diabetes is just not that severe," he told me. "Stop taking the insulin injections. It's far more dangerous for you to be taking insulin and sending your blood sugars so low than it would be to let them be a little bit high," he told me. "Take a break from obsessing so much about everything. And while you're at it, put your meter away as well and stop checking your blood sugars all the time." It was clear from what he'd said that he thought I had type 2 diabetes. And although he didn't state it, his tone let me know that he thought I was being neurotic, obsessive and verging on hypochondria.

I left his office as intimidated as I would have been if he were Jerry Robbins.

It was a spring day in New York City with birds chirping and cheerful people strolling. But as I walked down Park Avenue, I was unaware of my surroundings and more confused than ever. How could I have gone so far in the wrong direction? Was this doctor right? Did I have type 2 diabetes, after all? Could I stop taking insulin? Stop the blood sugar checks? Eat more carbohydrates? At that point I didn't know what to believe. It had taken all my willpower to convince myself that I had insulin-dependent diabetes. Now, was I supposed to convince myself I didn't have it?

I wanted to believe that I wasn't a severe diabetic. My longing to feel normal, that ounce of denial I still harbored, overcame my apprehension. "He's right," I told myself. "Stop being so neurotic. Let go, live, have fun again."

Soon, I was eating pasta, bread and fruit. I was going out to restaurants. I was eating the whole apple and not fretting about it, going to salad bars and actually eating crackers and bread with my tuna fish. It wasn't just the taste of the food I loved so much. It was the freedom of not having to calculate all the time. I loved not having to prick my fingers in order to check my blood sugars at every given moment, or poke myself with a syringe. I loved that I didn't have to worry before I went to bed. For a brief time I felt like my old self, smiling and laughing.

But not for long. The symptoms of high blood sugar returned almost immediately: the hunger, thirst, frequent urinations, infected blisters and brain fog. The moment those symptoms started, I should have gone straight to my meter and checked my blood sugar levels. But I convinced myself that this was normal because, according to my new doctor, it was okay for my sugars to be a little high. My denial was strong enough and my brain was foggy enough to maintain the delusion. I didn't just hate having a disease, I hated the way I handled it. I wanted to get away from the part of myself that had become so neurotic. And I was able to justify not picking up my meter by telling myself that I was following doctor's orders. As rigid as I had been about following my previous doctor's protocol, I was now equally rigid about never going back to taking insulin and possibly losing consciousness while I was dancing.

As much as I would have preferred to eat whatever I wanted, I knew that it was important to eat as healthily as I could. I had to get strict again about my diet. I believed in Grandma's diet, but Grandma wasn't there, and I knew that I did best when I not only followed a specific plan but also had someone to guide me through it. I remembered that one of the books I'd read when I was staying with my grandmother had been about macrobiotics and diabetes. I decided to give that a try.

I met with a macrobiotic counselor, who gave me a list of exactly what foods I should eat at every meal. She seemed convinced that I could control my diabetes with diet; she said she'd seen it done over and over again. Those success stories were all about people with type 2 diabetes, and that's what we all now thought I had. I decided to give it a try. The counselor gave me a list of foods and dishes I'd never heard of. To learn how to prepare them, I took cooking classes on Mondays when we had our day off. Soon I was pressure-cooking brown rice, sautéing burdock and lotus root, steaming my fish, boiling my carrots and putting ginger compresses on my pancreas. My diet was very high in carbohydrates, and even though they were the good, complex ones, without insulin, my blood sugars must have been hitting the roof.

I didn't feel well and I was becoming emaciated. What with the high blood sugars, the strict high-carbohydrate, no-fat macro-biotic diet, and my performing every night, my weight dropped to below ninety-five pounds—and I am almost five six. In addition, my skin turned orange from all the beta-carotene, and my muscles became stiffer and stiffer, to the point where no amount of massage brought relief.

My teachers at SAB, Suki Schorer, Susan Pilarre and Kay Mazzo, whose classes I still took, were noticeably concerned and constantly asking me how I was doing. Kay, who had been a great Balanchine ballerina, had just retired from the stage and joined the faculty of SAB when I first arrived. Now she is the co-chair of the school's faculty. She, in particular, knew what I was going through, because her own daughter had been diagnosed with insulin-dependent diabetes when she was just thirteen months old, and she was constantly urging me to see her daughter's doctor, Fredda Ginsberg. I kept assuring them all that I was fine. Since I was following my doctor's orders, that's what I chose to believe. I didn't think I was any thinner than other dancers who got a bit too thin, and I was dancing a full schedule. But of course I wasn't fine.

Before performances I'd go to Marika, the main company physical therapist, and wait until all the other dancers had been helped. Marika had such healing hands that as soon as she put her hands on my solar plexus my entire body began to relax. I appreciated her taking the time to work on me, but she could only give me temporary relief because, even though I didn't know it, my blood sugars were out of control. I tried not to let anyone see how much pain I was in, but I was so stiff that I looked as if I were wearing a corset and I could barely move.

I looked weaker than ever, and I was in so much muscle distress that I barely slept. I told my new doctor, but he didn't seem alarmed. He just prescribed sleeping pills that didn't work and that left me feeling drugged on top of everything else I was feeling.

Ninety-five pounds, looking, feeling and dancing like the Tin Man, I knew there was no way Peter would pick me for any new leading roles. Why would he?

I hated what my body was doing to my life.

TWENTY-NINE

I looked terrible and felt just as bad, but I was deluded enough, and determined enough, to decide never to go back on insulin, and I came up with any excuse I could think of *except* uncontrolled blood sugar to account for my worsening condition. Still convinced that I had somehow created my situation, I needed to come up with some way to un-create it. And I had no idea that I was endangering my life.

Among other things, I convinced myself that a big part of my problem was dancing so much. I was now twenty-five years old and had been with the company for seven years. Very often, corps dancers who have paid their dues, as I had, don't have to dance in every single ballet, and they get to perform more highlighted corps roles. They might even get an evening off here and there as the soloists and principal dancers do. I was getting some of those highlighted roles, but I was also dancing the simpler parts—I wasn't being excused from anything. Consequently, I was rehearsing all day and dancing in two to three ballets each night, and I believed that if only I could have an evening off to rest my muscles, I'd look and feel better.

Every day I thought of going into Peter Martins's office and explaining that I looked so bad because I needed an easier schedule, at least for a while. I rehearsed what I would say in my head, but how could I ask him to make me a special case? If he gave me nights off, my muscles might relax, but I'd be proving that I couldn't handle the workload and I could say goodbye to the hope of ever being given another solo role. I told myself to forget about being a soloist; just tell him the truth so I could enjoy being in the corps.

In the end, however, I just couldn't do it. Why couldn't I ask for what I needed? Partly it was because if I couldn't keep up, what was I doing in the New York City Ballet? Some dancers who were among the most favored did speak up when they needed a lighter load. But I didn't feel I had yet proved myself enough to deserve that privilege. And even if I did deserve it, I had other emotional issues that held me back. I still remembered the frightening repercussions of my having spoken up to Dave all those years before. And I still had the lingering fear of being seen as the "bad Zippora"—the problem child, the troublemaker.

Also, and equally important, as much pain as I might have been suffering offstage, when I was onstage I still had moments when I felt like a normal, functioning person, and I was still dancing those great Balanchine ballets. Should I continue to struggle and go for those moments in the hope that I might get better parts one day, or should I accept a lesser but more realistic alternative? That was my dilemma.

I knew Peter wouldn't fire me if I asked for special treatment, but would he suggest I join another company that didn't dance as many months and seasons? Most companies had shorter seasons than NYCB; some were only a few weeks long. But looking and feeling as I did, I couldn't imagine starting all over again, auditioning and proving myself. And, in any case, that's not what I wanted. I only wanted the repertoire I was dancing. Otherwise I'd rather quit dancing altogether.

Maybe that's what I needed to do. "This might be the right time to think about quitting," I told myself.

People quit all the time for one reason or another. Catherine, who was an extraordinarily beautiful dancer, was struggling with her weight and Jerry wasn't casting her in leading roles, either. Many corps dancers had decided to leave when Balanchine died and Peter took over. Talented, artistic dancers with their entire careers ahead of them had chosen to stop dancing and do something else because dancing wasn't working for them anymore. Even Suzanne Farrell finally retired in 1989 when a hip injury forced her off the stage after more than twenty-five years.

Why couldn't I do that, too? Why couldn't I go home to L.A. and go to college? I couldn't, because dancing with City Ballet was the only thing that still made me happy. But when I wasn't onstage, I wasn't happy.

I couldn't help comparing myself to the dancer I had been and lamenting my unrealized potential. Most of the dancers who had been in the cast of *Les Petits Riens* with me were now soloists, and although I was happy for their success, it was difficult to be left behind.

I knew I was drowning in self-pity, and I knew that compared to the majority of dancers, who wait tables at night to pay for their classes and who never get to perform, I was extremely lucky to be a member of one of the greatest companies in the world.

I understood all that. Even so, I was miserable, and needed to talk to someone.

There was one person I could go to: Susie Hendl. Susie had always taken a maternal interest in me. I knew she truly cared about my health issues and believed in my talent. In the fall of 1991, I took the chance and confided in her.

"I'm scared that this may all be too much for me," I told her. "Maybe this would be the right time for me to think about quitting. I know I'm not dancing well anymore. Jerry gave up on me long ago, and now Peter's giving up on me, too. Maybe I need to face the reality that I'm just not cutting it."

But Susie didn't want me to give up yet. She had an idea. Peter had recently choreographed a beautiful pas de deux, *Four Gnossiennes,* with music by Erik Satie, for SAB's workshop.

Afterward, he restaged it for the company, and it would be performed in the coming winter season. It was a beautiful and difficult piece, requiring a tremendous amount of control. I couldn't believe that Susie thought I would be able to do it. Did I not look as bad as I felt? She believed in me so strongly that she actually went to Peter and suggested he let me dance it.

* * *

The next week I was called to rehearse *Four Gnossiennes.* My partner, Ben Huys, was the dancer for whom Peter had choreographed it at SAB and who was now a member of the company. Ben was Romy's best friend from SAB. They even went to the prom together. He was a beautiful dancer with long legs and a pure line, and he was a great partner. We looked good together and I was thrilled to be dancing with him.

Susie told me afterward that Peter had asked her if she thought I could do it.

"Let me rehearse her," she told him. "Just give me plenty of time. You can come and be the final judge."

For the next six weeks, in addition to my regular corps rehearsals, Susie rehearsed Ben and me every day. *Four Gnossiennes* was the most controlled dance I had ever done. Peter's steps were incredibly difficult. The piece required the same level of control that I'd needed in the one turn I'd done in *Les Petits Riens.* Just when I wanted to go to the left, he would have me go against the momentum of my body to the right. I never felt I had mastered it, but with Susie's excellent coaching and Ben's great partnering, I was able to manage. The day Peter came to see it, everything worked like magic and we were cast.

The day before the performance, after my macrobiotic buffet of brown rice and root vegetables, I had an anxiety attack. The room was spinning and I was afraid to leave the apartment. I knew my sugars had to be rising because of the adrenaline my body was producing, but I didn't want to think about that. I wasn't willing to go back to testing my levels and taking insulin injections while performing. I told myself that my sugars would come down naturally when I began to dance.

During the performance of *Four Gnossiennes*, the calm I felt onstage equaled the anxiety I had felt the previous day. I was like a person dying of thirst who is finally given water. I drank it up.

After that performance, I didn't think any more about quitting. I had rediscovered my sense of purpose. I felt the magic again.

Still, I couldn't go on the way I was. I may have rediscovered my love of dancing, but I hadn't come to terms with the fact that I was sick, and getting sicker.

In July 1992, when the company went to its summer home in Saratoga Springs, I rented a house with my friends Jeff and Catherine and went swimming at nearby Lake George on weekends. Even though we were still rehearsing and performing, everyone seemed to be more relaxed in Saratoga.

That summer, my weight hit an all-time low. One night in the dressing room, one of the other corps dancers came up to me and told me that I looked terrible and needed to gain some weight. She was really nasty about it. Did she think I'd lost all that weight on purpose?

Another night, as I was warming up for the performance, I overheard two dancers talking about me.

"Does she think it looks good?" one asked.

Couldn't they see I was standing right in front of them and

could hear every word they said? Did it even occur to them to ask if I was okay? No. They just assumed that I was anorexic.

I had hoped that being out of the city might help me relax, maybe even to get a good night's sleep. Instead, I was just as edgy and suffering as much from insomnia as I had been. Then one night shortly before we were due to return to the city, I did manage to fall asleep for a few hours. But I was shocked back into wakefulness by a terrible dream. I'd had nightmares before from time to time, but this one was different. In the past I'd always woken up just before I died. This time I didn't wake up. Instead I saw myself dead. I'd never died in a dream before. And it didn't feel like a dream.

Like the dream I'd had in which I was suffocating in the car, this one was a wake-up call. Suddenly, just like that, I knew I was on the wrong path. I knew I needed to check my blood sugar levels. My life could be in danger. I would have done it right then, but since I hadn't been using it, I hadn't brought my meter with me. For some reason it didn't occur to me to go out and buy one. Instead, even though I was terrified, I told myself that I'd check my sugar levels the moment I got back to the city.

Two days later, I rode the bus back to New York with the rest of the company, dashed to my apartment, threw my bags down and searched frantically for my meter. It must have been at least a year since my last finger prick. When I finally found it, I pricked my finger, pushed the blood onto the strip and waited for the beep. The meter showed three thin lines. I didn't recognize the symbol.

Where was my instruction manual?

I searched my drawers, telling myself it was probably a symbol indicating that the batteries were low. I opened the manual and flipped to the page explaining what the different symbols meant. There, I read the words, "This meter does not go up this high."

How high do meters go? Six hundred? I tried not to panic. I had no insulin. Sitting there in my apartment, I realized that I had become my own, self-created disaster.

"Help me, God, please," I said aloud, "help me. I don't want to die!"

THIRTY

I remembered that Kay Mazzo had given me the phone number of her daughter's doctor, Fredda Ginsberg. I'd never called, but, thankfully, I'd held on to it. Terrified, I called Dr. Ginsberg's office and was told to come in immediately. I was back on insulin that same day.

I felt as if I'd been living in the spin cycle of a washing machine for more than two years. By that time I was exhausted.

I trusted Dr. Ginsberg immediately and was ready to accept that I needed the insulin. It wasn't going to be easy, but I'd finally learned my lesson. At this point my fear of dying from not taking it far outweighed my reluctance to admit that I was, and always would be, a person with type 1 insulin-dependent diabetes.

I'd already stopped being so strict with my macrobiotic diet while I was in Saratoga, and it was harder to stick to my routine. I knew that not all macrobiotic diets were as strict as mine in any case, so I gave myself permission to start eating more fat and protein and fewer carbohydrates.

With the insulin, my sugars came down immediately, and within a month or two, my blood sugars normalized and so did my weight. The good news was that I was getting healthier and no longer ignoring what my body was telling me. The hard part was that, once again, I had to learn to juggle shots of insulin with my schedule, and that wasn't any easier now than it had been the first time I did it. The difference was that this time I was going to be smarter about it and learn how to do it properly.

Certainly I looked better and was dancing better than when I wasn't taking insulin, but I couldn't help asking myself if I was crazy to try to dance all day and perform every night while trying to walk the tightrope of balancing my blood sugars with insulin injections. Was it really worth it? I had to ask myself if I was being realistic. Maybe I needed to admit that I'd had a good run in the world of George Balanchine and Jerome Robbins and the time had come to graciously bow out.

Although Peter Martins had been pleased with my performance in *Four Gnossiennes* and cast me in the role a number of times the following season, he was clearly hesitant to consistently cast me in leads the way he would someone whom he was grooming for promotion. Once again I was tired from dancing so much, and I was emotionally exhausted from trying so hard to prove that I was the same dancer I had been before I was diagnosed.

With brief exceptions, like the nights I danced *Four Gnos-siennes,* I was not the same. Performing in the corps de ballet night after night, I felt that I had drifted further and further from the pure, expressive dancer I once was and longed to be.

Once again I thought about scheduling an appointment with Peter Martins and announcing my decision to leave. And, at the same time, I tried to analyze my true motivation. Had I finally come to terms with the reality of my situation or was it a cop-out? I'd get to the theater each morning wondering which path I was going to take—down the hallway to Peter's office or the one to the main rehearsal hall. Every day I'd be in the rehearsal hall and every night on the stage, wanting just one more ballet, one more chance to experience the greatness of the world I was in. For months I struggled, and all the while I tried to figure out why I couldn't just make the decision.

Finally, I arrived at a moment of clarity. I'd been telling myself that I was tired of the struggling with insulin doses and blood sugar ups and downs, but in truth I wasn't just tired of struggling with diabetes. I was more tired of constantly struggling to become the dancer I might have been. I was tired of feeling that I wasn't living up to my potential.

While dancing was better than not dancing, I wasn't experiencing the innocence, elation and purity of heart I once had. Although those moments onstage were still the times when I felt most alive, they were also the moments that reflected to me the dancer I had been and wasn't any longer.

I told myself that I hadn't been on the right diet and insulin regime for very long. I had to give my new routine a chance to work. If I left before I did that, I would never know how much I could really achieve. I had to give myself that opportunity. I made a commitment to myself to give it more time to find out what was possible. If I tried everything I could, if I gave it enough time, and if it still was too much for me, that would be the time to quit. But first I needed to confront my fears and frustrations and see what I could do.

THIRTY-ONE

As it turned out, I was right not to quit. Almost as soon as I made my decision, things began to improve in large ways and small. Finally I had found a doctor with whom I felt comfortable and whose balanced approach to diabetes was one I could live with. I was in the embryonic stage of learning how to dance with diabetes, but already I looked better, moved better, felt better, and my weight had returned to thin but healthy.

I was taking two kinds of insulin. My short-acting insulin, which worked within two to six hours, was to be used before meals and whenever my sugars were too high. Today, short-acting insulin works in just fifteen minutes.

In the evening, I also took long-acting insulin, which remained in my body for up to twenty-four hours but which wasn't as consistent as the long-acting insulin we have today. Rather than providing a continuous, even output, it often kicked in with a surge, lowering my sugars at various hours of the day and night. Since I couldn't really predict how the lingering effects of all the exercise I'd been doing would affect my system, it was difficult to know how much I should be taking. I'm a light sleeper, and night after night when I awakened in the small hours, I'd check my blood sugar and, if it was low, drink some juice and wait for my levels to return to normal.

Low blood sugars were still a constant concern because they were so dangerous. High blood sugars, on the other hand, affected my ability to dance well. Both affected my ability to enjoy what I was dancing.

Sometimes, before a performance, I'd mistake the shakiness of anxiety for the shakiness of low blood sugar. Sometimes the adrenaline rush caused by pre-performance nerves caused my sugars to rise. When that happened, I would have to make a judgment call as to whether or not I should take a shot. Many factors went into making that decision: How high were my sugars? Were they dangerously high, or just high enough to make me feel spacey and out of touch with my body? How aerobic was the ballet I'd be performing? How large was the role I was about to dance?

Some roles required much less stamina and output of energy than others. How many times would I be exiting the stage? If I had a lot of breaks I could check my sugars and make sure I was okay, or eat something sweet if I wasn't. Some roles, however, kept me onstage throughout the entire piece, which meant that I didn't have an opportunity to do that.

Most of the time, I resigned myself to having a higher blood sugar than I would have liked. In consequence, my blood circulation was sometimes impaired, my body wouldn't be as warm as it could or should be, and I would lose that exquisite connection I needed to have with every part of my body in order to perform at my highest level. But I was no longer trying to be perfect. The best I could do would have to be good enough.

Even though it wasn't easy, it was worth it. I was beginning to feel like a semblance of my old self onstage again. My insulin regime seemed to be working, but because of my ever-holistic approach to health, I believed I could do more to help my progress with a good diet and proper supplementation. I was still having sleep problems, and my muscles still hurt more than I thought they should. As usual, I was reading everything I could find on the subjects of diabetes, insomnia and athletes. I also read about vitamins and herbs that help conditions like sleeplessness and muscle pain. I finally found out that people with diabetes are more prone to higher levels of lactic acid, which causes the burning you feel during and after a workout. Fluctuating blood sugar levels can also make it more difficult for oxygen to get to the active muscle. Now I understood why I was in such pain. The question was: what could I do about it?

There were so many vitamins and herbs to choose from. How could I be sure that I was taking the right one or the right combination? I knew I shouldn't try it all on my own.

At about the same time, a friend told me about a doctor who practiced a form of holistic medicine that I had heard very good things about. Dr. G practiced out of the apartment he shared with a woman who was both his life partner and his assistant. On my first visit, I filled out a long form on which I listed all of my ailments. Dr. G explained his treatment program, which involved baths and massages with various oils, specific drinks and herbs, as well as a specific diet designed especially for me, which would first detoxify and then rebuild my body. He said he could help with all my problems. It sounded great, and I agreed to give it a try.

In the past, except for Grandma, I'd never felt that anyone had given me the support I needed to figure out how to implement whatever protocol they'd prescribed. As a result, left to my own devices, I'd continually wound up going overboard in the wrong direction.

Dr. G appeared to be interested in every aspect of my well-being and was totally available to help me. No more trying to figure out which vitamin was good for my diabetes, which herb might help me sleep. He gave me supplements and worked by my side, following my progress on a daily basis, teaching me how to cook the dishes that were best for my body. He took me to the market and introduced me to many new foods. Previously, when I'd tried to cook the foods on my macrobiotic diet, I could never be sure I was doing it correctly. Now, the doctor invited me to come for dinner, and he prepared the meals while I took notes. I loved the food he cooked and loved learning such exotic recipes. I started to relax and didn't feel so alone. The doctor and his girl-friend and I became good friends. But our relationship wasn't always completely comfortable.

I sometimes felt that Dr. G was a little *too* available. I couldn't exactly put my finger on what was bothering me, but something just didn't feel right. Still, for the first time I was feeling like myself again, and I wasn't about to allow what could have been nothing more than my own imagination to keep me from working with someone who was there for me and really helpful. So I just tried to put it out of my head.

That turned out to be a big mistake.

By now my mother, Romy and I were all living separately, and even though I was sleeping better on Dr. G's regimen, I was still afraid to be alone at night. I couldn't help worrying about what might happen if my blood sugar went too low and my body didn't wake me up. What if I took an herb to go to sleep and relaxed myself so much that I didn't wake up when I was low?

This was a real concern, since over time people with diabetes sometimes develop what is called hypoglycemia unawareness. Their body becomes so used to lows that when one occurs the body doesn't signal that something is wrong.

Since I lived alone and didn't want a roommate, Romy thought that, at the very least, I should adopt a cat. On our day off, she took me to the ASPCA. It seemed that the cages held either litters of newborn kittens that I couldn't imagine separating from one another or cats that were fully grown. But finally Romy saw a four-month-old black cat alone in a cage and looking scared. She took her out and held her. Then she put her in my arms.

We took her home and I named her Kayla. I hadn't bonded with an animal since Gent, so it took Kayla and me a while to get used to each other. But once we did bond, I never wanted to be without her. Anyone who has ever bonded deeply with an animal knows how important it can be in your life.

Like many animals, Kayla truly had a sixth sense and often seemed to know when my sugars went too low. Today, dogs are trained, using their sense of smell, to sense changes in blood sugar levels and alert their owner. There are also new devices that alert you whenever your blood sugar is too low or too high. But those devices didn't exist at the time, so Kayla became my sensor. There were many nights when Kayla nudged me awake with her paw, and I'd force myself to get up and check my sugars. Invariably when she did that, I'd see that I was low and I'd go to the kitchen and eat or drink something sweet.

Not only was Kayla a great companion; she was a potential lifesaver.

THIRTY-TWO

With my new doctor and insulin regime, Dr. G's diet and supplements, and Kayla's potentially life-saving company, I seemed to be back on track and I was enjoying dancing more and more.

While Peter Martins had been casting me as Sugar Plum every winter and giving me a few other leads, they'd been few and far between. Then, in the spring of 1992, when I'd been seeing Dr. G for only a few months, he cast me for the first time in Balanchine's *Apollo*.

Mr. B had created many masterpieces, but none that I loved more than *Apollo*. Set to the music of Igor Stravinsky, Balanchine had created it 1928, when he was just twenty-four years old, and would later say that it was the turning point of his life. The ballet tells the story of the young god Apollo and the three Muses—Terpsichore, the Muse of dance, Polyhymnia, the muse of mime, and Calliope, the Muse of poetry—who vie for his attention.

The first *Apollo* I saw was danced by the legendary Edward Villella, who, along with Jacques D'Amboise, had made it cool for men to be ballet dancers. An Al Pacino look-alike, Eddie came from Brooklyn and had actually been a boxer for a while. He was tough and athletic and executed leaps and turns that made audiences gasp. But he was also an artist, who could bring everyone in the theater to tears. Although he'd already retired from City Ballet when I arrived at SAB, I did get to see him dance a solo from *Apollo* once when I was a student, and he invited me to go with him on a lecture tour he'd organized. Young as I was then, I recognized that his performance was spectacular.

Nordic blond Peter Martins was physically Eddie's opposite, but when I saw him dance the same role opposite Suzanne Farrell's Terpsichore, he, too, was everything I'd ever imagined a god to be.

My Apollo would be Peter Boal. Margaret Tracy would dance Terpsichore, her sister Kathleen would dance Polyhymnia, and I would dance Calliope.

It was an honor for Peter to have included me in this new young cast, and, as it had been for Balanchine, *Apollo* was also a turning point for me.

From then on, I performed the role many times that season and in the years to come. Whenever my mother was in the audience, she beamed as she always did when she saw me or Romy perform. On one occasion, I also invited Dr. G, who had seen me dance before but never in such an important role. I was happy to have him in the audience because I truly believed that he—along with the insulin—was the reason I was feeling so much better.

* * *

I continued my treatments with Dr. G twice a week. I was happy with my progress, but there were times when his behavior really bothered me. Once, after I'd had dinner with him and his girlfriend, I told him I'd been having a hard time sleeping and needed to get home. He asked if he could help me relax for a bit before I left. Why didn't I say no?

While his girlfriend cleaned up the dishes, he took me into the extra bedroom and tried to hold me and rub my back while we lay together. I felt repulsed and angry that his supposed attempt to nurture me was so totally manipulative.

Still, I didn't tell him what I was feeling. Instead, I thanked him politely and went home, wondering how many women in my situation had fallen for his come-on. What did his girlfriend think we were doing? He must have had some sort of understanding with her.

After a while my muscles were less sore and I was sleeping better, but there was still one problem that was bothering me. Like many dancers and athletes, I wasn't getting my period regularly. I had discussed this with my medical doctor and even tried several rounds of hormone therapy, but the hormones had made it more difficult to control my blood sugars, and I hadn't been willing to take on that added burden. I'd mentioned the problem when I started seeing Dr. G, and now I asked if he could focus on it.

He told me then that he'd been including possible remedies

in the treatments and supplements he'd given me throughout the year I'd been seeing him. These treatments and supplements were all he had to offer, and since they weren't working, he had something else to recommend.

"What's that?" I asked.

If I wanted to get my period, he said, I have to start having sex.

"I don't have a boyfriend," I replied, slightly annoyed. "And I'm not going to have sex as a prescription for getting better." Dr. G then suggested that if there was no one else available, I should have sex with a friend.

"Like who?" I said, suspecting what his answer would be.

"Like me," he replied.

Because I'd spent so much time with Dr. G, he and I had become friends, and I knew enough about him that I also knew he'd had relationships with women he was treating as patients, so I wasn't completely stunned. Until that moment, however, despite the uncomfortable evening when he'd rubbed my back, I still hadn't realized that I was to be his next conquest.

Still, the idea that he was using my not having a period as an excuse for getting me to sleep with him was totally disgusting and offensive. I flat out told him that I wasn't attracted to him. If that hurt him, I didn't care. He was out of line and I was trying to make light of it.

"Oh, c'mon," I said. "Give me a break."

We dropped it for that session.

I should have walked out of his apartment right then and never come back, but I didn't.

* * *

The advances continued for many months, and each time I tried to make a joke of it. I wished he'd stop, but having to push him away seemed a small, if annoying, price to pay given the benefits I was getting from his treatments. He was the first person to have taken such an interest in me, and for that I was grateful. So I kept finding ways to rationalize what he was doing. What was so wrong with his being attracted to me? Given what I'd felt about my body, shouldn't I be glad that somebody was?

I was convinced the reason I didn't have a boyfriend was that, since I'd been diagnosed at the age of twenty-one and my body fell apart, I'd been too ashamed and disgusted with myself to attract anyone special. But having a boyfriend, someone to connect deeply with in an emotional as well as sexual way, was really important to me.

I'd had many blind dates and introductions from friends, but I'd always felt more alone afterward than I did before the date. I was looking for someone who wanted to be with *me*, the young woman struggling with a disease, not the glamorous ballerina everyone seemed to expect me to be.

One guy that I met for lunch had spent the whole time asking what great parties had I been to, and whether Jerry Robbins had been at any of them.

At least Dr. G knew about my diabetes and my sleep problems and still really liked me. I was so desperate to be healed that I forced myself to stop being repulsed by him. I couldn't help it. I deeply believed that his treatments were the reason I was doing so much better, and I was afraid to let go of him—and them. Yes, I had just begun a regular insulin regimen, as well. But, as I saw it, without Dr. G, I wouldn't have been doing as well as I was. The need I felt for him was so great that, in the end, I was willing to put up with whatever he did.

I'd probably been slightly depressed at times in the past but I hadn't felt serious depression until the week before my twenty-seventh birthday.

Something about turning twenty-seven and still being alone triggered a well of hopelessness in me. I was convinced that I would never find anyone to love who could love me in return. While I had always wanted to have a boyfriend, I had never before felt such an intense longing. I couldn't pull myself out of it as I went through my days in a fog.

I didn't want to see Dr. G, but I had promised him I'd come over for dinner that week. One evening when I was only dancing in the first ballet and would, therefore, be finished by nine o'clock, I was feeling so down and so tired that I just couldn't muster up the energy to cook for myself, so I decided to have a good meal with him.

I didn't say anything about what was bothering me, but he must have picked up on my state of mind and realized that my guard was down.

I honestly don't remember how it started. After we ate, we were sitting on his sofa. I remember him being next to me and then somehow behind me. He started to rub my neck. Then his hands were on my breasts. Passively, I let him keep doing it, and that was his green light. Before I realized what was happening, he was kissing me and then he was taking my clothes off. I wasn't enjoying it, but I told myself he might be right. Maybe this would help me. I was sick of myself and my problems. Maybe having sex with him would change my energy; maybe I'd be more attractive once I'd had sex. At least I knew him and we were friends.

He started to enter me. He'd been after me for such a long time, and finally he was getting me. I hated every minute of what was happening, but still, I was allowing it—until, all of a sudden, something snapped me out of my stupor. No matter how much this person was helping me, this was horribly wrong. I had to get out of there. I pushed him away and told him I had to go home.

He tried to convince me to stay. But I was out the door.

When I got back to my apartment, he'd already left a phone message. I didn't call him back. I was as disgusted with myself as I was with him.

A few days later, I had enough distance from the immediate event to confront him and communicate my feelings instead of running away. I went back to his apartment and told him that his behavior was inappropriate and I couldn't see him anymore. He tried to tell me I was wrong to leave, that what had happened wasn't such a big deal. He went on about "Americans" and our "sexual hang-ups."

Afterward, he continued to call me off and on for the next few months, but I never saw him again.

The hardest thing for me to accept was knowing that I was as responsible as he was for what happened between us. Having known that he'd had sex with other women he'd treated and that he was trying to get me into bed, I had been sure that I could handle it. So how did I end up so down and depressed that I could no longer resist his advances? I had read that blood sugar fluctuations can affect your emotions and thought processes. Is that what had happened to me? If not, how could I possibly explain to myself why I'd lost all perspective? How could I have thought that I could improve my life by having sex with someone I didn't want to have sex with?

Yes, it was true that because of him (or so I thought), I was dancing better than I'd danced in years and I was afraid to lose his support, but that was no excuse for losing myself.

THIRTY-THREE

Once I let go of Dr. G, things started heading in a direction I could never have anticipated. As it turned out, all of my fears about losing his help and advice were unfounded. In fact, I discovered that I was stronger and healthier than I'd thought.

Now it was time for me to take responsibility for myself and work with my doctors. I needed to become a full member of my health-care team.

I also needed to stop lamenting and start appreciating where I was in my career. Yes, I might be in the corps de ballet for my entire career, and yes, I'd hoped for something more. But I had accomplished a lot. I was successfully balancing insulin-dependent diabetes with dancing as a member of the New York City Ballet. Even though my salary was modest, I was able to support myself in New York City, making my living from something I loved. How many people could say that? It was time to stop blaming myself, to trust in myself and be grateful.

I now understood that many factors must have contributed to

my contracting diabetes: genes, environmental factors, stress and quite possibly a virus. Yet I still believed that I had done something to bring the diabetes on, that it was my fault, some terrible karma. It was time to stop thinking that way and to have more compassion for my body and for myself.

If I could accept that I was not perfect and that my blood sugars would not always be balanced during my performances, I could be more patient with myself. If I did these things, I could go a long way toward understanding that true health is about more than a physical state of being; it is an awareness and acceptance of one's body. I could learn to live with diabetes and be at peace with the way that my life was unfolding.

Interestingly, it naturally occurred that as I came to accept myself as an imperfect dancer, enjoying every moment and grateful that I had not given up, I also became more interested in what lay beyond the world of the New York City Ballet.

As it happened, a number of professors at Fordham University were offering to teach classes on Monday evenings, making it possible for NYCB dancers to take college courses on our one day off. Romy and I, along with many other members of the company, signed up for the program. Over the next several years, I would take one course per semester. In time, I studied English, chemistry, art history, biology, math and psychology. Taking those courses expanded my mind and my soul.

At the same time, I was also becoming involved with Continuum Movement, a new modality created by a former dancer named Emilie Conrad that was based on a series of wavelike movements affecting different systems and parts of the body, including the circulatory system. When I practiced those movements, I could feel the oxygen getting to my muscles, which relaxed as I spiraled and undulated. In time, through daily practice, I would later come to love these movements as much as I loved the experience of dancing on the stage.

As I was expanding my horizons, something else extraordinary happened to change my life even more. Some people say you find love when you stop looking for it. I wouldn't say I'd ever stopped looking. I'd just stopped looking for it as a way to feel complete. Ironically, it wasn't long after I left Dr. G that I met the man with whom I would spend the next five years.

Ulf and I met dancing in *The Nutcracker* in Amarillo, Texas. Peter Boal and I had been invited as guest artists to dance the roles of Sugar Plum and her cavalier with a regional company/ ballet school. Ulf was also a guest performer dancing the Arabian Prince, a role for which he was perfectly suited. He was tall—six two—German by birth but more Scandinavian in looks. He had blond hair and blue eyes, a dancer's body and an artist's soul. I noticed him immediately. He was so gorgeous, how could I not? I tried not to stare, thinking that a man as handsome as he would never be interested in me. During the performance, I watched his dance from the wings as I warmed up in preparation for the grand pas de deux. He was commanding and mysterious, completely lost in his character. I was so impressed that when I found myself standing near him after his dance, I leaned toward him and took his arm. "I wanted to tell you how wonderfully you did. You were great." I whispered loud enough for him to hear over the music for the "Waltz of the Flowers."

He looked surprised. "Can I talk to you sometime?" he asked. "I'd love to get some advice from you."

"Sure," I replied, but I didn't have much time. Peter and I were the guest stars and hadn't flown in until the last minute. At that point, we'd only be there for two more days, and we had plans for both evenings. I told Ulf that Peter and I were being taken out to dinner by our hosts after that night's performance, but I could meet him after dinner if he didn't mind that it would be late.

I knew we were in the same hotel, so it was easiest if he just met me there.

"Why don't you come to my room?" I said. I was tired and figured that would be the easiest thing for me. It didn't occur to me that he might find me attractive or assume anything more about the invitation than what I had meant.

"Should I bring anything?" he asked politely.

At the time, I was drinking dark beer to unwind. Dr. G had suggested it and it seemed to work, so just because I'd given up Dr. G didn't mean I had to give up my Guinness stout.

"Sure," I told Ulf. "Bring some beer."

I was so naive at the time that it didn't even occur to me that I might be sending out a sexual signal. I was just trying to find a good time to talk, and I could use a beer.

Ulf, on the other hand, told me later that he'd assumed I was this hot ballerina who was used to having guys come over to her room and sleeping with them. When he showed up at midnight with the beer, he was clearly nervous. It was late, I was exhausted, and we had two shows to dance the next day. When I started asking him questions, he quickly realized he could relax.

I sat on the bed and he sat on the floor with his back against the dresser. I could tell he liked me, and I liked talking to him—so much that we talked until 5:00 a.m. We could have talked longer, but I had to get at least a couple hours of sleep. Except I couldn't sleep; I was excited. This guy was not only gorgeous, he was intelligent, interesting and had the heart of a poet.

After our final performance, I figured that I'd never see him again. I had no idea where he lived, and I thought this was goodbye. But I was wrong.

As it turned out Ulf was living in New York and was actually going to be on the same plane as Peter and I.

On the flight back to New York, Peter and I sat together. Ulf was several rows back. He wrote me sweet notes and gave me his phone number. I really liked this guy, and his actions told me he felt the same way. I knew he would call.

Back in the city, Ulf wanted to see me every day. If I had an hour or a rare evening off, he was waiting at my doorstep. I wanted to be swept away, but I was a guarded person and it wasn't easy for me to fall blindly in love. I was afraid Ulf would get discouraged, but as it turned out, Ulf needed me as much as I needed him.

A month into our "courting," which consisted mainly of hanging out in the park or at my apartment, he came to me one evening scared and concerned. He was in New York on a student visa so he wasn't allowed to work. He was doing some catering from time to time off the books, but he wasn't earning very much money. Now he was being kicked out of the room he'd been renting and he couldn't afford anything else. He had nowhere to go, no one to turn to. Would I let him live with me? If not, he would have to go back to Germany.

I felt enormous pressure. I wasn't sure if I could let this person I hardly knew move in with me, but I wasn't prepared to lose him either. I was finally in an intimate relationship. On the one hand, although I was excited about the chances of my having a future with this man, I was not prepared to start living with him yet. On the other hand, I had waited my entire adult life for a relationship, feared I'd never find someone to love, and had even let my doctor take advantage of me.

Back and forth I went. After everything I'd been dealing with in terms of my health, was I ready to have someone in my space, my one-bedroom apartment? I worried about whether I would still be able to do what I needed to do to maintain my routine and continue dancing with diabetes. But I knew that Ulf was passionate about health. He loved to cook organic and healthy meals. We were compatible in many ways. The more I had come to know him, the more comfortable I felt. I said he could move in.

In the years to come, we shared great times and much love. In many ways we grew up together. This was the first real long-term relationship for both of us. I learned a lot from Ulf, but it wasn't always easy.

As with every relationship, there were areas of tension and compromises to be made. I had wanted someone who was interested in the offstage me, and that's what I got. But I didn't anticipate how hard it would be for him that I spent so much time at the theater and was home so little. He resented the long hours, the toll dancing took on my body, what I was going through with my health, and, most of all, the time it took away from us.

For my part, I was learning for the first time how to have an intimate relationship, and, at the same time, I was dealing with my own health issues. I needed to figure out how much I could reasonably share with him about what I was going through on a moment-to-moment basis. How much should I involve him? How much should I tell him? We lived in a small one-bedroom apartment. There was no way that he wouldn't hear my meter beep or see me at the refrigerator at odd hours. Should I tell him every time my sugars were either too high or too low?

I'm not one to hide anything. I wanted him to know why I was shaky and why my mood might suddenly change. But because I still tended to be hard on myself, it was easy to get testy with whoever happened to be around when I was annoyed with myself. My tone was sometimes snappish or condescending when I didn't mean it to be. When I was exhausted, it wasn't just from dancing all day and all night, it was from being high or low all day and night. I wanted him to understand that, but I didn't always say it nicely. I was still angry at myself and still working on trying to show myself more compassion.

THIRTY-FOUR

I'd been with Ulf for about a year when rumors started to circulate throughout the company that promotions would be announced toward the end of the spring season. For me, this season was different from the others. As much as I was grateful I hadn't quit sooner and was enjoying my days and nights, if I didn't get promoted, I was now prepared to move on.

Although dancing was still my passion, I could see myself continuing only if I had the opportunity for full artistic expression, which would come only if I were made a soloist. Without that opportunity, I no longer had the will to put myself through everything I needed to do as a person with type 1 diabetes just to get myself onstage.

On the day promotions were announced, the chosen dancers were called, one by one, into Peter's office, and told the good news. One dancer's promotion was announced over the backstage loudspeaker in the middle of a rehearsal. I heard nothing, loud or otherwise. I spent the day congratulating other people and trying to look as if I didn't care, although it was obvious to some of my friends that I was being passed over. When they came up to me individually and said they were so sorry, I held back my tears.

The day seemed to drag on endlessly, and by late afternoon all I wanted to do was get out of the theater, go home, have a good cry and start to figure out how I would move on with the rest of my life.

All of this was spinning through my mind as I dressed to go out and get a snack before the evening's performance. I was just getting up from my dressing table when Peter's secretary came over to me.

"Peter wants to see you. He's in the theater," she said.

As I made my way down to stage level and into the theater, I was so prepared to deal with my disappointment that I was almost wishing he wouldn't have good news.

Peter was sitting alone watching a final rehearsal. As soon as he saw me, he stood up and threw his arms around me.

"Congratulations!" he said. "You're a soloist."

Then he studied my face for a moment. I don't know if I looked annoyed or relieved or amazed or if it was just that he could see I'd been stressed.

He smiled. "Did you think we forgot you?" he said.

So, that was it. Six years after my diagnosis, in my ninth year with the company, I had been promoted. I walked out of the theater reflecting on my long journey. I thought about how I'd tried to hide what I was going through, how much I'd wanted to be able to function in this world where, although we were delicate, we were also strong, resistant and tough. Had I really become what I was so determined to be? As a soloist, I'd consistently be given roles in which I could express myself and grow. Could I now relax, knowing that I would be nurtured and fulfilled? One of my remaining concerns then—as it would always be—was whether I could continue to function at the level I expected of myself.

THIRTY-FIVE

Being a soloist was, in fact, everything I had dreamed it could be. I was being given new and wonderful roles to dance. Performing them night after night brought me to a level of comfort onstage I had not experienced as a corps dancer who did featured roles only from time to time. Although as a soloist I had the added pressure of always being "out there" and exposed, not being able to hide among the rest of the corps, I was confident enough to take on that pressure. I was proving, not only to myself but also to Peter, that I was strong, consistent and could maintain the ballerina's lifestyle while taking insulin. Now I just had to be in the moment and enjoy what I had achieved.

Still, I had to be vigilant and responsible about taking care of my health. Each day was different, but after so many years, I'd found a general routine that worked for me. Most important of all, I had to check my blood sugar levels throughout the day, before every rehearsal and numerous times before the performance.

I needed to rely on my monitor and make smart decisions about when to take a shot. Psychologically, I also needed to accept the fact that I wouldn't always have a great performance, and that was okay because it was better to let my sugars be a little high than to risk a low blood sugar by taking a shot.

I always started my day with a hot shower because the water soothed my aching joints. If my feet were really sore, I'd soak them for ten minutes in Epsom salts and then dust them with powder to keep my toes dry.

One of the most important things I had to do as a person with diabetes was to take care of my feet. Like all dancers, I was constantly getting blisters and corns from the rubbing of my pointe shoes, and occasionally one would become infected. Although the infections weren't caused by diabetes, they—like the terrible sores under my arms when I was dancing *Petits Riens*—took longer to heal because of my poor circulation. While my poor circulation may or may not have been related to my diabetes, higher blood sugar levels along with poor circulation make wounds and sores slower to heal.

It had taken me years, but I'd finally realized that, in addition to controlled blood sugar levels, as soon as an infection started, I needed to stay off my feet. It was hard because, as always, I feared being seen as someone with injuries, and all dancers are always performing with corns and blisters. So, in the early years, I'd dance on the infection, which meant that it got so bad I'd be at risk for an infection that could spread into the bloodstream or an amputation if the sores didn't heal. Eventually it would get bad enough that I'd have to go to the doctor, who would then order me to stay off my feet, and the healing process would take longer than if I'd done the right thing in the first place. After a while, I learned that missing a performance or two when I first got an infection was better than dancing on it and then having to miss a couple of weeks.

One of the things that helped to prevent me from getting infections was always wearing white cotton socks under my point shoes in class and in rehearsals, and changing them throughout the day. Another precaution I took was always to wear flip-flops when I showered in the group dressing room. Most dancers wear adhesive tape or Band-Aids on their toes to protect them from blisters and corns. I was especially careful to do this, and to put moleskin and corn pads anywhere there was uncomfortable pressure from wearing a tight shoe all day. Sometimes I actually cut a hole in the shoe, which wouldn't be seen from the audience, to try to relieve the pressure.

One of the luxuries of being in a company is having toe shoes fitted to your feet and made to order. My shoes were made exactly to fit the specifications of my feet, and I was constantly changing the specifications, trying to find the perfect fit. It was a long process that never ended in all my years in the company.

As a soloist, I shared a dressing room with four other soloists. We each had a dressing space where we applied our makeup. We also each had a black theater case that was always left open, where we stored our clean tights, trunks and pointe shoes for that evening's performance. Beyond that, there were massive amounts of pointe shoes and rehearsal clothes strewn all over the room.

When I arrived in the morning, I'd change from my street clothes into my leotard and tights and head up to the studio for class. Some dancers don't need as much time, but I always needed at least thirty minutes to stretch and warm up my body before I was ready to start moving. The first plié of the day was always hard for all of us. Some dancers sighed, we all giggled, everyone ached from the night before, and it helped to know we were all experiencing it together.

By the end of class I'd worked out my soreness and was ready to give my all in rehearsals, which lasted from noon to 6:00 p.m. with an hour break for lunch at some point. Since we never knew when that break would come, I always had food in my dance bag—dried fruit for lows and nuts and seeds in case I was too hungry to make it through to the lunch break.

Sometimes, when I didn't have a full day of rehearsals, I might even get a few hours off in the afternoon. In that case I would go home for lunch, relax and spend some time with Ulf before heading back to the theater to put on my makeup, re-warm-up my body, and then perform. If I was just in the first piece in the program, I might be home by nine-thirty and could have a nice dinner with Ulf. But if I were on last, I might not get home until close to eleven-thirty.

Looking back on that time, I sometimes wonder how any of us could have kept up with that schedule day after day. There were occasions, after a day of class and rehearsals, when all I wanted to do was go home and collapse just at the time when I needed to summon up an even higher level of energy for the evening's performance. But then I would remember the inspiration and energy boost I got from the backstage atmosphere—the musicians warming up, the stagehands getting ready, dancers changing into their costumes—as I was preparing to go onstage, not to mention the sheer excitement and joy of the performance itself.

Different dancers have different pre-performance routines for warming up. Mine began at home when, if I had time, I would visualize myself the way Suzanne Farrell had taught me so many years before. I would see in my mind exactly how I wanted to dance, including all the details that would be necessary for giving a great performance. At the theater, I would make sure my body was thoroughly warmed up. I always did a nice, long warm-up even though I'd had class and rehearsals all day. Finally, in the ten minutes before the curtain went up, I'd go out on the stage, where I'd do the actual steps over and over until I felt comfortable with them and my body was extremely warm and ready to go.

Sometimes, when I was particularly nervous, I'd picture Sheila, the way she held her chest up, how overflowing with enthusiasm she was. I forced myself to remember why I was there, to love my experience, to not be afraid of imperfection. I reminded myself how many dancers would never be given this opportunity. I could not let my nerves rob me of being as great as I could be. I could not let my excuses, my fears, even if they were valid, interfere. I would not!

Each day I had to go out there and dance to the best of my ability as a soloist with the New York City Ballet. If coping with diabetes was an added factor in my ability to achieve that, taking care of my health was also my responsibility. Except for checking my sugars, taking insulin or eating something sweet if I needed it, I never thought of myself as being different from any other member of the company. I never used my diabetes as an excuse. In fact, I went to the other extreme, never letting anyone except Ulf and Romy know what I had to do to get myself out on the stage and dance well.

One of the things I especially loved during my years as a soloist was working with new choreographers and, especially, having someone create a role specifically for me. One of my cherished experiences was working with Lynn Taylor-Corbett, who has choreographed not only many ballets for various companies, but also hit Broadway shows including *Titanic.* Her ballet *Chiaroscuro* was a mood piece featuring the phenomenal Jock Soto, with five other dancers coming in and out of his "dance." Lynn had a clear vision of each character, and she wanted me to dance one of them.

During my six years as a soloist, I was cast in roles I never thought I'd be privileged to dance, ballets that had astounded me with their beauty and grace when I was a student and a young corps de ballet dancer. One of the most memorable for me was Balanchine's *Liebeslieder Walzer,* in which I was once again partnered by my close friend Ben Huys.

Another highlight of those years was dancing in the 1993 celebration Peter Martins had arranged to commemorate the tenth anniversary of Mr. B's death. For this event, the members of City Ballet were joined onstage by leading dancers from the world's premier companies.

I was honored that, for the celebration, Peter chose me to dance the pas de trois of *Agon* with Kathleen Tracy and Peter Boal. This is one of the thirty-three ballets that comprise the epic collaboration between Balanchine and Igor Stravinsky, and, like all Balanchine ballets, it is a work of movement wedded to music. Balanchine wasn't trying to tell a story. "Dancing," he said, "isn't about anything except dancing."

No two parts could be more different than the fierce and fiery role I danced in *Agon* and the classically graceful Sugar Plum Fairy. Unless I was injured, I was cast in Sugar Plum every *Nutcracker* season until I retired.

As the years passed, I became more nervous dancing Sugar Plum in her beautiful pale green tutu than I was about any other role. When I was young, it was easy and exhilarating to step into her gracious heart. I experienced her as not only gracious but also pure and wise, one who appreciated and respected every creature in her kingdom.

Although it was always one of my favorite roles, and I believe that I grew technically and artistically in the part, with time and age also came more and more self-consciousness and doubt. I was worried that I couldn't live up to what I'd once been in the role. Once I stepped on the stage, my fears disappeared and the dancing took over, but not without a week or so of extreme anxiety and sleepless nights.

In truth, I always felt pressured when I danced in a tutu. Because of the stiff bodice, you can't move as freely in a tutu as you can in a leotard, and even though my body was suited to a tutu, I felt extremely constricted and boxed in. For that reason I always preferred leotard—or fully skirted ballets—and whenever I danced Sugar Plum, I pretended that I was dancing in a leotard. In the end, despite my nerves, it was always a joyful experience.

By the mid 1990s, when I was promoted, City Ballet had changed in significant ways from the time I joined the company. It was now Peter's company and he was making it his own. The year I was promoted, he let go of many older corps dancers who had worked with Balanchine and developed their work ethic and aesthetic from him. At the same time, many other dancers—including some that Peter very much liked—left the company unexpectedly. In the wake of that exodus, the composition of the company changed dramatically.

The women and men who had worked directly with Balanchine were slowly disappearing. Gone were Suzanne Farrell, Patricia McBride, Ib Andersen and Karin von Aroldingen, and, inevitably, other dancers were dancing their roles. At first it was difficult for me to watch other dancers performing their signature pieces, but I came to appreciate that different dancers brought something special of their own to these roles and that this is what kept the ballets fresh and new. When Balanchine was alive, he had continually created new works that kept the company dynamic and alive.

But he had always maintained that when he was dead, he did not want City Ballet to become a museum. Besides the new ballets that were being created, part of what kept it from becoming that was seeing new dancers reinterpret roles he had created.

The company's ranks were being filled with dancers of my own generation, artists of great talent who were now coming into their own, bringing their own special gifts, experiences and emotions to every role they danced.

In January 1996, Lincoln Kirstein passed away. This was a huge loss and his absence was deeply felt. Then, two years after Lincoln, Jerome Robbins died.

Even though Jerry had long ago stopped casting me, he hadn't stopped noticing me. Whenever he passed me in the hallway, he would make it a point to stop and ask about my health. I always appreciated his attention and particularly remember the day, long before my promotion, when he came over to me while I was warming up my muscles before a rehearsal and said, "I've been watching you from the audience, trying to figure out what it is. Don't think so much about the audience. Get more into your body. Just be inside it."

I was incredibly touched that he had taken the time to figure out what was keeping him from using me. As a rule, Jerry didn't do that for people. He didn't have to do that for me. I knew what he meant. At the time, my muscles were in so much distress that they wouldn't respond. As a result, I was having to put so much energy into my performance that I was probably overperforming. Although it was embarrassing to know that my trying so hard had looked to him as if I were trying too much, I appreciated the fact that he cared enough about me as a person to try to understand why he was disappointed in me as a performer.

Although I'd never really worked directly with Balanchine, and Jerry had never nurtured me in the way I'd hoped he would, I was, nevertheless, touched and influenced by their presence and their genius. Throughout my career, older dancers told me how sorry they were that Balanchine passed away before I had really gotten to work with him. As the years went by, however, I came to appreciate what a blessing it had been to work with him even for a moment, to have witnessed him, and to have had the privilege of working so closely with the people who had spent their lives working directly and intensely with him. I was lucky enough to have come in at the tail end of what was a period of astounding creativity and a confluence of larger-than-life talents and personalities in the world of dance.

Now the culture of City Ballet was changing in many ways. In keeping with the times, the atmosphere of the company had become less formal, and while that meant that a certain element of mystique and glamour was lost, the company also felt more familial and comfortable.

Although I didn't know it at the time, and I would continue to perform for six more years as a soloist, I was also changing, finding a new path for my future and my life after performing.

While I was taking courses at Fordham, I had thought that I

might someday do something in the fields of health or psychology. I had never thought about teaching dance for a living after I retired, but I had always enjoyed teaching at Sheila's studio whenever I went home to L.A. Now I was finding that I loved coaching, as well. When Romy performed and I wasn't onstage, I would watch her from the audience or from the wings and give her advice if she asked for it. Sabrina, the long-legged dancer from Julio's Gyrotonics class, had also become a close friend, and she, too, often asked for my feedback. I was amazed to discover how much information I actually had. To my own surprise and delight, I discovered that simply by watching them move, I could figure out what worked best for them and find ways for them to execute steps more easily and beautifully. Maybe this would be a way for me to stay connected to dance when my own dancing days were over.

PART SIX

Off My Toes at Last

THIRTY-SIX

Looking back, it sometimes seems that I'd spent my entire career thinking about when to let go, but now the time had really come. I was ready. I had been in the company for sixteen years. Over the course of those years, I had suffered common injuries: ankle sprains, knee problems, hip problems. Although not one of them was career-ending, cumulatively, they had taken their toll.

The most profound experiences of my life had come through dance. For my sixteen years with City Ballet, dance had been my focus. Whether I wanted to admit it or not, my self-definition, my identity, had been wrapped up in being a dancer. That was now changing. To continue dancing at the level I had been, my commitment would have to be absolute, and it wasn't anymore. By this point I regarded dancing as "what I do"; I no longer saw it as "who I am."

Whatever came next, I realized, I would experience myself in a new and interesting way. I was ready for this. More than ready. It wasn't that I no longer cared about performing. I still loved it. But my path had taught me to accept changes. It had taught me to be open to the unknown with all of its remarkable possibilities.

One significant change that directly influenced my decision-making process was the fact that my relationship with Ulf had ended and I had begun seeing someone who lived far from New York.

I had thought Ulf and I would be together forever. Every relationship has its compromises, but we loved each other. After five years, however, we were growing further and further apart, and even though we were still living together, we were fighting more than we laughed. Ulf was a romantic. For all the years we were together, he not only wanted to be as important to me as my dancing, he wanted our life together to be the *most* important thing. He simply didn't understand why I couldn't leave the stage, why we couldn't move someplace else, live with the land and grow our own food. For years, I hadn't been ready to leave, and by the time I was getting to that point, it was too late for us.

I met Kip at a psychologically based spiritual workshop I took when the company was on a two-week break. I didn't go there with any thought of meeting someone new, nor did Ulf, at the same time, go to Germany to film a television series with any thought of meeting another woman. But it happened for us both. Maybe we were both ready to really find love with someone else.

Although Ulf had always supported me whenever I brought up the idea of retiring, I had never felt that he truly supported my life as a dancer with City Ballet. Truthfully, I didn't think he liked the part of me that was driven to perform at that level. He loved me, but he didn't want me to be pushing myself so hard. He didn't understand why it was so important for me, and he saw the toll it was taking on my body. I felt that understanding immediately from Kip, because he was a performer himself and knew what it was to have that burning desire to be at the top of your profession. I hadn't fallen immediately when I first met Ulf, but for whatever reason, I fell hard when I met Kip.

When I first noticed him in the workshop, I had no idea what he did; for all I knew this dark and long-haired, handsome man could have been a gas station attendant. But he wasn't. Kip turned out to be a double-platinum-selling rock musician who had gained his fame in the eighties during the big-hair band craze. While I was doing *tendus,* he was living the life of a rock star. But he knew what a *tendu* was more than most, having taken ballet himself.

I didn't think he'd notice me, but I was wrong. He did notice me, and we had dinner together the last night of the seminar. The next morning, Ulf called me from Germany. He had been with another woman but was sorry and wanted to come home to me. "I just met someone," I told him. There was a long silence.

I had planned to meet Ulf the next week in Germany. I had no idea what was ahead with Kip; I didn't even know if he'd call me when I returned to New York. But I knew it was over with Ulf. We both knew it. I did meet him in Germany, and when we returned he started looking for an apartment.

Ulf moved out, and Kip, who lived in Santa Fe, did call me back.

We began a four-year long-distance relationship. Kip understood who I was on every level. He was in tune with me artistically, emotionally, mentally, physically and spiritually, and I was in heaven. For the first time in my life I even lost my appetite. Happy or sad, I had always eaten. But this was different.

Kip would fly to New York whenever he could and I would fly to him whenever I had a break in schedule or had to take time off because of an injury. Although we wanted to be together, we both knew that I had to keep dancing until *I* felt it was time for me to leave. Once I left, there would be no going back, and I never wanted to wonder if I could have done more. I didn't want to regret the decision once it was made.

As our involvement grew my heart was increasingly pulled away from the stage. Finally, my life offstage began to feel as important as my life onstage. For more than a year, I carried on a dialogue with myself about whether I should stay or go. Ultimately I accepted the fact that the emotional core of my life wasn't onstage anymore and that, in any case, my body had already made the decision because I was becoming injured more and more often.

My last performance for City Ballet was in the role Lynn Taylor-Corbett had created for me in *Chiaroscuro,* but very few people knew it. Except for my closest friends and, of course, Peter Martins, I hadn't told anyone I was leaving. By then I'd been spending more and more time in Santa Fe, and I'd been injured a lot, so many people had probably gotten used to my not being there and assumed that I was leaving. But, for whatever reason, I chose to go out quietly.

THIRTY-SEVEN

As my own life was changing, so were the lives of my family. Grandpa Jack had passed away soon after the birth of his first great-grandchild, Shoshana, who was the first of six children born to my sister Michele and her husband, Paul.

Romy and Catherine left the company four years before I did, and both moved back to California. Catherine attended Stanford University, where she met her husband and started her family. Romy married her longtime boyfriend, Alex, and moved back to Los Angeles where our mother would move, as well. Soon, Romy gave birth to a son, Gabriel. My brother, Gary, and his wife, Sarah, also began their family.

As for me, I moved out of the city and moved in with Kip. At first, all I wanted was to take some time to rest and reflect, to be a normal person who actually had time for a romantic relationship. I had met someone who gave me the possibility of a full life without the stage, and I was looking forward to it.

After twenty years of getting up, taking class and rehearsing all day, I luxuriated in not having to wake up at a specific time, get myself to the theater and push my body through morning class. It was an important choice for me to not get a job right away, so that I could relax and recuperate from a lifetime of dancing. I did, however, begin teaching a couple of days a week at a local ballet school and enjoyed my minimal involvement with the world of ballet.

I hadn't really figured out what I was going to do next, but I wasn't immediately concerned. So many years of being told where to stand and how to stand and dissecting every little movement had taken their toll on my psyche. At the moment, it felt good just to "be," with no pressure and no expectations. At night, I'd dream I was in rehearsal taking direction or getting corrections before a performance. Suddenly I'd turn to Rosemary, the ballet mistress, and yell, "I won't do it anymore."

What did concern me a bit was the possibility that my sugars would go up without the constant exercise. As it turned out, they did go up some, but not as much as I'd feared. I maintained a healthy eating plan and continued a daily workout consisting of Continuum movement, yoga, ballet stretches and barre exercises. The most immediate and noticeable improvement was in my ability to sleep. Not exercising at night, eating dinner and going to bed earlier helped me to unwind and stay asleep longer.

For the first time I was able to really give myself to a relationship. While my relationship with Ulf had been great for a long time, I had never been entirely available in terms of either emotions or time. Between my schedule and my diabetes, I'd had two full-time jobs.

Now I was available, present, and I was exactly where I wanted to be. The truth is, I never looked back. I didn't miss my days at the theater. My closest friends were no longer there. My mother and Romy were both back in California, and I spoke to them on the phone every day. I was glad to be in a life that felt exactly right and to think about what was next for me.

I had not, however, cut my ties to Balanchine completely. When I was leaving the company, one of the few people I told was Susie Hendl, who was on the board of the George Balanchine Trust.

The Trust was established in 1987 to preserve and protect Balanchine's great ballets. Today it is headed by Barbara Horgan, Balanchine's former personal assistant, Susie Hendl, Karin von Aroldingen and Kay Mazzo.

It had never occurred to me that teaching for the Trust was something I should even inquire about, but when I called Susie, she said, "You know, I think you would be really good at staging ballets. Why don't you give it a try?"

Balanchine ballets are danced all over the world and are a vital part of the repertory of every major and regional company, many of which feature all-Balanchine programs. When any dance company, or any school anywhere in the world, wants to stage a Balanchine ballet, they must get permission from the Trust, which then assigns and sends what is called a *répétiteur*. The *répétiteur* teaches all the steps in a given ballet, and coaches and directs the ballet in the manner Balanchine intended it to be danced.

Dancing Balanchine requires tremendous speed and attack, the latter being the ferocity with which you use your legs and the energy you put into every step. It can be quite challenging to dancers trained in different styles, although it's equally exhilarating and freeing.

When Susie made her suggestion, I felt torn. Not only did I want a break from what I'd done for so many years, but also, having struggled so hard to be perfect, I didn't want to inflict that dynamic on anybody else. I didn't yet know that I would have a gift for helping to unlock other dancers' potential and help them feel good about themselves while they were striving for excellence.

Susie, however, wasn't letting me off the hook. She persisted, and I really wasn't in a position to turn down a paying job. I met with Barbara Horgan, and a few months later she gave me my first assignment: staging two ballets for Goucher College.

You don't have to be a professional dancer to dance Balanchine, and the Trust has always been incredibly generous about allowing his ballets to be experienced by many levels of dancers, including those at ballet schools and universities.

The first ballets I was assigned to teach were *Concerto Barocco* and *Serenade*. I'd had the honor of dancing leading roles in both of them. *Serenade* was one of City Ballet's signature pieces, and it had always been one of the Balanchine ballets I cherished most.

Interestingly, Balanchine had originally choreographed it for

SAB students in order to teach them how to dance together on a stage and how to shine while dancing as an ensemble. It is a unique work, into which the amazingly adaptable Balanchine incorporated random events that had occurred in the studio. One day a student fell and he put that in. The day male students showed up, he worked them in, as well. On another day a girl came late and this, too, became part of the ballet. Later, asked why he had used seventeen girls in the opening sequence, he said it was because that was how many showed up the day he was choreographing that section.

I had danced *Serenade* for many years. The music and steps were in my body and, beyond that, in my soul. Only now I would be responsible for knowing the counts and steps for every dancer, corps as well as principals. Karin von Aroldingen lent me her handwritten notes in which she had specified all the patterns, steps and counts for every single part. There were sixty-six pages of notes and I studied all of them, then watched videotapes of different performances over and over again and took my own notes. I danced around my living room until I felt comfortable with each person's role.

Balanchine often changed the steps to accommodate different dancers; maybe this ballerina had a better extension to the front with her right leg while another was better with her left. The beauty of a live performance is that every night and each cast are different. Did the dancer in that video intend to go in that direction? Was a particular move choreographed or was it a spontaneous decision? Or could it have been a good-looking mistake? Balanchine encouraged his dancers to express their individuality. Performances from one year had different patterns at various places than the same ballet performed in a different year. As the *répétiteur,* I was now responsible for deciding which version was best suited to the dancers I was directing.

It was a privilege and an honor for me to be able to impart Balanchine's brilliance and greatness to these younger dancers who were, for the most part, experiencing his magic for the first time. From the first step I taught, I knew I loved teaching and coaching. I loved the looks in these young dancer's eyes when I showed them the step; I loved seeing their elation when they danced them. This was not about being perfect; it was about the joy of dance.

It moved me to realize that my years of dancing Balanchine's ballets and working with the greatest teachers had enabled me to become part of that vital, creative chain of individuals who pass ballet along from one person to another.

THIRTY-EIGHT

A year after I stopped dancing and left New York, my relationship with Kip ended. It wasn't my decision, and even though I knew that I, too, bore some responsibility, the breakup left me feeling bereft. It had always been through dance that I had been able to sort through my feelings. Dance had helped me through every major event in my life. Without it, I had to face an emptiness I'd never before experienced. I felt lost.

I no longer had a life or a job in New York, which had been my home for twenty years. Los Angeles wasn't a place I had thought I'd ever live again, but my entire family was there. My mother had moved back a few years before to be closer to her grandchildren and was now living around the corner from Romy. When I asked if Kayla and I could come stay with her, she didn't hesitate for a moment. I'd never needed her love more than I did then. It was the place I needed to be.

Now that I was alone again, I also needed and wanted to work. I needed something to focus on to keep me sane. I called Susie at the Trust and let everyone I knew who taught ballet that I was ready and willing to work. One of my friends from City Ballet was soon to be the new director of the Norwegian National Ballet, where I subsequently flew to teach company class and lead rehearsals. Ib Andersen had become the director of the Arizona Ballet, where I also staged ballets and taught company class for months at a time.

Over the years, the Balanchine Trust has continued to give me work, and I have had the honor and privilege of staging Balanchine ballets throughout the United States and in many other countries.

I never thought that anything would be as important to me as dancing. Nor could I have predicted how much meaning I would find in working with other dancers and giving back.

While I myself was struggling, I had been too busy hating my struggle to see beyond it. Teaching, more than anything else, made me grateful that I hadn't given up. The lesson I had learned about persevering is one that I now pass on to my students. We all experience rejections, we all have failures; the point is to learn from them, to move through them, to continue to grow and thrive.

At the time I moved in with her, my mother was still working as a physical therapist. She'd rub my feet after I'd been teaching all day and I started to rub her back. Not one to complain, she had been suffering back pain that she assumed had been caused by lifting a patient, and I was hoping to help her feel better, as she had helped me on so many occasions. Beyond that, neither one of us thought much about it. We certainly didn't think it was anything more serious than a muscle strain.

It was about a year later, while I was in Sweden rehearsing a Balanchine ballet, that Romy called to tell me she had taken Mom to the emergency room in the middle of the night. Apparently while Mom was asleep my cat Kayla had been kneading on her the way she often kneaded on me when I had low blood sugar. Mom woke up gasping for air and barely able to breathe. In the hospital the doctors drained her lungs, which had filled with fluid. Then they ran a series of tests.

Two days later, I finished my work in Sweden and went straight to the hospital. Soon, there was a diagnosis: cancer. It would be a few weeks more before we learned the worst: the cancer had eaten away at her rib, hence the pain in her back where I was rubbing. My mother had stage-four lung cancer with six to nine months to live.

I stopped traveling altogether and taught only at the local ballet school so that I could be totally available to her. It was as if everything I had been through was preparing me for this moment. Finally, my own health struggles stood me in good stead, helping me to be present for my mother and to understand that she was incapable of knowing which decisions to make in light of such a dire diagnosis.

Michele, Romy, Gary and I, along with my father and both my aunts, pulled together, educated ourselves and worked as a team. Since I was the person living with her and the one most able to devote my time and my life to her care, I took the lead. Since her diagnosis was terminal, we took chances and followed unorthodox protocols as well as traditional ones. We got her to the right doctors and I got her on a good diet. In short, I did for her everything that I had done for myself.

She lived three more years—three good years with new grandchildren and her loved ones around her. Even though I'll always wonder if I could have done more and wish that I could have had her longer, I feel deeply grateful for the time I had with her and the unconditional love we shared.

THIRTY-NINE

As far as my own health was concerned, I'd been blessed, since moving back to Los Angeles, to find Dr. Anne Peters, a professor of medicine and director of the USC clinical diabetes programs and the author of *Conquering Diabetes*. A doctor whose compassion and understanding are as extraordinary as her medical expertise, she is a healer in the truest sense of the word.

I found her name in a newspaper article about Gary Hall Jr., an Olympic swimmer who'd been diagnosed with diabetes and was told that he would never be able to swim competitively again. The article went on to say that when Hall consulted Dr. Peters, she was as determined as he was to at least give it a try. With her by his side, he went on to win ten Olympic medals before retiring in 2008.

The article was accompanied by a photograph of Dr. Peters standing by the pool Hall was training in. I only wished that I'd had someone like her standing in the wings while I was performing. Today, there are diabetes educators whom you can call for help at any time of the day or night. They were around back then, too, although there weren't as many as there are now, and, in any case, I didn't know about them. If I'd had that kind of constantly available source of information and support, I believe it would have made a big difference for me.

When I finished the article, I called Dr. Peters's office, and she's been my doctor ever since.

While I was still performing, several articles had been written about me in different diabetes publications and I often teamed with the Juvenile Diabetes Research Foundation to bring kids to see me perform. Afterward, I'd speak to them about how I took care of my diabetes and I always enjoyed inspiring these children and encouraging them to follow their dreams. But I was too consumed with my life as a performer to give any more than that.

Everything was different now. I was feeling ready to do more, and to give more. As happens so often in life, one thing has serendipitously led to another, and doors have opened when I least expected them to.

Dr. Peters introduced me to Dr. Steve Edelman, founder and head of a nonprofit organization called Taking Control of Your Diabetes. He invited me to be the keynote speaker at one of their conferences, where, for the first time, I spoke in depth about my experiences of dancing with diabetes. Like with teaching, I instantly found meaning in sharing my story, and motivating and connecting with others.

For these events I have created a series of movements that are fun and easy and that anyone can do. Many people with diabetes don't exercise, so I like to show them how good it can feel to move their bodies to music. We start small but I encourage them to keep at it, and to incorporate some sort of movement into their daily lives. It's another way for me to pass on the gift of dance that I've been so privileged to have.

My friend Kari Rosenfeld introduced me to Children with Diabetes and to Novo Nordisk. Children with Diabetes is a wonderful nonprofit organization that provides information and support to children and teens with diabetes and their families, and with which I have had the pleasure of working for many years now. Novo Nordisk is a world leader in diabetes care and working with them I've traveled all over the world, from South Africa to Israel, sharing my story.

I have also worked closely with Dr. Francine Kaufman, a past president of the American Diabetes Association, a professor of pediatrics at USC and the author of *Diabesity*, a fascinating book about the relationship between obesity and diabetes. Fran is an amazing and dedicated physician who has inspired my advocacy work, and who has helped me reach thousands of children and teens with diabetes.

Through these dedicated healers and educators, I have been given the opportunity to write another chapter in the book of my own life. As a dancer, I had expressed myself through my body. Now I was learning how meaningful it could be to use my voice in order to share my story. From that first talk I gave at the TCOYD conference, I felt a great sense of purpose, and in the years since, it has become one of my greatest passions. Instead of hiding my struggle, as I had for so many years, I am now using it to connect with people and help give them hope as to what they, too, can accomplish if they take proper care. And I am using my love of dance to get people up and moving.

It has been especially fulfilling for me to see how meaningful it is for children and teens to meet someone who has been able to persevere and go on to lead a passionate life with diabetes. For many kids having diabetes is a label they live with, something that sets them apart from others. To help counteract this feeling, I do one exercise I call Stand Tall and Proud, where I have kids lift and stretch as tall as they can, and to let their breath fill up their bodies as they walk around the room. It's a great sight to see a group of kids prancing around like this, and I tell them not to be afraid to "take up space"—conveying the message that diabetes is nothing to be ashamed of.

The teenage years are among the most challenging—with or without diabetes. I especially enjoy doing movement with this age group because they seem to especially appreciate my honesty. At an age when everything is so dramatic, adding diabetes to the mix only compounds the anxieties of adolescence. When I share my story with these kids they see that I, too, struggled with my illness, and I don't gloss over this to my "happy ending." Most of all, though, I think they see that having diabetes doesn't mean their life can't be normal, which is what so many teens strive for. I show them that it's possible to be happy, and healthy, and that having diabetes shouldn't stop them from doing anything they want in life.

* * *

When I began to speak about my life, I didn't want my story to just be "girl overcomes obstacles to live her dream." It was important to me to discuss and share my diagnosis, my denial, my fears and all the hurdles I encountered, and I have been amazed to see how many people are affected and motivated by my story.

One of the hardest things to do is motivate other people. What I say to those with diabetes is equally applicable to anyone who has encountered an unexpected obstacle or whose life path has not turned out to be what he or she expected.

My message is simple: Passion is what motivates us and gives our life meaning. My passion for dance gave me a reason to be healthy. Each one of us needs to find our own passion in life and use that to motivate us to take care of our health.

Never let anyone tell you that diabetes will stop you from what you love, but don't—as I did—put your heath at risk for the sake of achieving success.

Try not to think of exercise and following a healthy diet as things you *have* to do because you have diabetes. People with diabetes are not cursed while every other person gets to pig out on banana splits. Everyone needs to eat right and exercise. Find ways to move because it feels good; maybe just turn on some music and dance around your living room or bedroom like you did when you were a kid. I know it's not always easy. But try to remember how lucky we are to have devices and therapies that help us live full and passionate lives. Be healthy and keep moving in your heart and on your feet. Get enough rest and take care of your emotional health.

Live your dreams, live your passions, let this life be full of meaning and connection and don't let anything stop you. Your passion could be a profession, or it could be simply spending time with your loved ones, playing with an animal, smelling the roses or all of the above. Whatever it is, anything you care deeply about can inspire you to take better care of yourself and make your life matter.

Remember that when your blood sugars are too high or too low it's easy to get stuck in habit patterns that will keep you from realizing your goal.

Try to eat as healthfully as you can (I focus on organic foods) and by all means get enough sleep. As a result of my own sleep problems, I've come to recognize how important it is to do whatever you can to get the rest you need for optimum emotional and physical health.

Equally important, find doctors you trust and with whom you are comfortable communicating. Among other things, this means making sure that your doctor is educating you on the most recent advances in the field and discussing with you the best protocols for your particular situation. Given my own unfortunate experiences, I never envisioned that my medical team would one day be such an important part of my life or that my relationship with my doctors would become so meaningful.

And finally, I hope that everyone has the opportunity to discover how meaningful it can be to bond with a pet. My cats— first Kayla and now Marley—have brought me both joy and comfort. Today, Marley puts me to sleep with her purring. While

Kayla had a knack for warning me of a low blood sugar, Marley has a knack for helping me sleep.

While I will always teach dance, much of the work I do now is with diabetes. My hope is always that hearing what I was able to accomplish despite my struggles and doubts will motivate people to look at their own choices, take charge of their health and live life to its fullest.

Dance taught me how to give my heart and soul to everything I do. It taught me to take chances even when that meant falling down. It taught me, when I did fall, to get up, move on, and even shine. It taught me to value every moment, that journeys are as important as results; it taught me how to keep my balance. It taught me to let go, let the moment take over and let the magic happen.

Yes, my life was difficult, but without that experience, I could never have become the person I am today.

There are, of course, certain areas in which I'll always be working to improve—balancing my sugars, handling stress, eating as healthfully as I can and communicating better, whether in an intimate relationship, professionally, or with my doctors. Still, I'm grateful that I've come so far with so few repercussions. Because of my mistaken belief that taking insulin was somehow an admission of failure and my stubborn refusal to take it, things could have turned out very differently. I now understand that insulin saved me, as it has saved countless others before and since.

Each time I give a talk, I appreciate anew that my illness took me on a path I can now value and cherish, even though I hated being on it at the time. I recognize that in the midst of struggle, we all feel alone. Yet, in talking to others, I see how universal our feelings really are. It's the sharing of those feelings that provides the strength to move forward. Diabetes is a day-to-day, hour-to-hour disease, and that means that it can be exhausting. It's hard to always stay in control and feel that you're doing what you need to do. Knowing that others are having similar experiences is comforting.

I'm not saying it's easy and I'm not saying I wouldn't jump for joy if there were a cure found tomorrow. But I can honestly say I feel blessed to live in a time when there are so many resources that allow me and so many others to live full, healthy, passion-filled lives.

Recently, I found a couple of refrigerator magnets that had belonged to my mother and are now on my own refrigerator door. One reads, "The person who says it cannot be done should not interrupt the person doing it." The other reads, "I do believe that for every door that closes, another will open...but these hallways are really a drag!"

I keep walking toward the open door.

* * * * *

RESOURCES

I hope by telling my story that I have been able to encourage others to take responsibility for their health so that they can make good decisions about how to take care of themselves and live full and passionate lives, even with serious conditions. While we cannot control why certain things have happened, we can control the way we move forward and react to those circumstances. The following is a list of resources that I've found to be especially helpful.

BOOKS

If you or someone you love has been diagnosed with diabetes I recommend you read the following books:

Peters, Anne, M.D. *Conquering Diabetes: A Complete Program for Prevention and Treatment.* Plume, 2006.

Kaufman, Francine R., M.D. *Diabesity: A Doctor and Her Patients on the Front Lines of the Obesity-Diabetes Epidemic.* Bantam, 2006.

Specifically for Women:

Jovanovič-Peterson, Lois, M.D. *Managing Your Gestational Diabetes: A Guide for You and Your Baby's Good Health.* Wiley, 1994.

On Healthy Eating:

Pollan, Michael. *In Defense of Food.* Penguin Press, 2008.
My grandmother would have loved this book, which preaches "eat food, not too much, mostly plants."

Kessler, David, M.D. *The End of Overeating: Taking Control of the Insatiable American Appetite.* Rodale, 2009.
If you are having problems with food addiction and blaming yourself for it, this book points out how certain foods trigger addictive eating, and how educating and training yourself can help to avoid them.

DeRohann, Ceanne. *Recipes for Love.*
This wonderful cookbook provides recipes that are easy, inexpensive and healthful. It can be ordered at: www.rightuseofwill.com/recipes.htm.

WEBSITES

If you have just been diagnosed with diabetes, these Web sites are great resources:

www.diabetes.org

1-800-DIABETES

The American Diabetes Association has a Web site full of helpful information as well as a call center if you'd like to speak with someone in person. They also have a bookstore stocked with everything you need to know about managing diabetes and they publish a monthly magazine, *Diabetes Forecast.*

www.tcoyd.org

Taking Control of Your Diabetes (TCOYD) is a not-for-profit organization dedicated to informing and empowering people with diabetes to become actively involved in their own health care. Their wonderful conferences offer the latest information and helpful tools on how to manage diabetes.

www.childrenwithdiabetes.com

Children with Diabetes is an online community for kids, families and adults with diabetes. It is a fantastic place to get informed and motivated, and connect with others. Created by a concerned father of a daughter with diabetes, the Web site has a wealth of information, including the latest diabetes research, online chats, discussions and seminars with a faculty of prominent leaders in diabetes.

www.jdrf.org

1-800-533-CURE

Juvenile Diabetes Research Foundation (JDRF) is the leader

in research leading to a cure for type 1 diabetes in the world. It sets the global agenda for diabetes research, and is the largest charitable funder and advocate of diabetes science worldwide.

www.sansum.org

Under the leadership of Lois Jovanovič, M.D., Sansum Diabetes Research Institute is a research center devoted to the prevention, treatment and cure of diabetes. It is an extraordinary place, where diabetes research, nutrition, education, and diabetes prevention have improved the lives of people worldwide who suffer from this serious disease.

www.idf.org

The International Diabetes Federation (IDF) is committed to raising global awareness of diabetes, promoting appropriate diabetes care and prevention, and encouraging activities toward finding a cure for the different types of diabetes.

www.ndep.nih.gov

1-800-438-5383

The National Diabetes Education Program (NDEP) is partnered with the National Institutes of Health, the Centers for Disease Control and Prevention, and more than 200 public and private organizations, including the American Diabetes Association.

www.diabeteseducator.org

A diabetes educator is great to have in addition to a doctor. The American Association of Diabetes Educators (AADE) is dedicated to providing members with the tools, training and support necessary to help patients change their behavior and accomplish their diabetes self-management goals.

www.dlife.com

This is a great Web site packed with helpful information, personal stories, recipes and interviews with prominent figures in diabetes. They also sponsor dLife TV, a weekly 30-minute show for people with diabetes shown on CNBC.

www.nih.gov/health/infoline.htm

Whatever your diagnosis, the National Institutes of Health can connect you with helpful information.

www.diabetesincontrol.com

A weekly e-mail newsletter that summarizes and delivers the most critical information for diabetes medical professionals from over 200 journals, peer-reviewed scientific papers and studies.

The following nonprofit organizations are making a difference in the lives of people with diabetes around the world, and always need support:

www.insulinforlife.org

Insulin for Life is dedicated to providing adults and children with diabetes supplies in areas of the world where they are in emergency need. My personal friend Stewart in Zimbabwe has benefited from their outstanding efforts. I cannot thank them enough for the work that they do.

www.lifeforachild.idf.org

IDF has a program called Life for a Child, which supports the care of close to 1,100 children in over 18 countries worldwide. The program meets the children's immediate needs (insulin, syringes, monitoring and education), builds local capacity and lobbies governments to establish sustainable solutions.

ACKNOWLEDGMENTS

I am a dancer, a teacher, a movement motivator and a speaker. I never thought I would write, nor did I feel an inner calling to do so. When I began this process of writing my story, I knew I would need guidance and help, and this book would not exist without the support, patience and encouragement of many people who all deserve my deepest gratitude:

My agent, Barbara Lowenstein: you believed in my story from the beginning, knew where to take it, guided me and stuck by me as I learned over and over how to best express myself. Thank you.

My wonderful editor, Deborah Brody: you guided me through this process with patience and support, and you, too, believed in my story and helped me get it right. A heartfelt thank-you for your time and expertise.

The gifted team at Harlequin: without all of you this book would never have happened.

Elizabeth Kaye: your words on the page dance; you are as

beautiful a writer as you are a person. Thank you for the endless hours of writing and dialoging, and for helping me get my story on the page with grace and honesty. I have enjoyed every moment.

Judy Kerns: I could not have completed this without you. You are brilliant, patient, a pleasure to work with, and saved the day once again. Thank you.

Denise Ritchie, my loyal friend: thank you for all your help, especially in the beginning of this writing process. You are an endless well of insight and love and a blessing in my life.

Debra Greenfield: thank you for your unwavering belief in me, for your generous help as I began this process, and for bringing me to Elizabeth. May we always share the joy of dance together.

Elizabeth Kendall: thank you for your help with the finishing touches on this book, and throughout my dancing life.

Dr. Anne Peters, Dr. Francine Kaufman, and Dr. Lois Jovanovič: you are all great doctors and great women who inspire and guide me. Thank you, Anne and Fran, for your expertise regarding the medical information in this book, and Lois, for suggesting I send my proposal to Barbara, who became my agent.

As a dancer I'd like to thank the many teachers who influenced the artist I became, specifically Sheila Rozann, whose love of ballet opeed to me a world beyond anything I ever dreamed.

The writing of this book aside, I would not be where I am today psychologically and emotionally were it not for the many special friends I am so blessed to have in my life. To my closest and dearest friends, I hope you know how much you mean to me and how you help guide my life every day. While I cannot name you all, I'd like to thank Kari Rosenfeld, Laura Behr and Hanna Wise Heiting for your constant ear and feedback.

And to Steve Postell: with deep respect for your support and detailed help at every stage of this book, most notably the final read, and in admiration of your brilliant mind, caring heart and great music.

To my father, Allen, my stepmother, Lynn, and all my siblings, nieces and nephews, aunts and uncles, cousins, and all their significant others—thank you for always supporting me, no matter what I do or could have chosen to become. A special mention to my dad, whose compassion and wisdom guides me more and more each year.

Along with my father I'd like to specifically acknowledge my sisters, Michele and Romy, my brother, Gary, and my aunts Rhonda and Arlene. We came together for mom's illness, each in our own way, and I cannot adequately express the depth of my gratitude to you. Mom deserved only the best.

And lastly, a special thanks to Romy. We grew up in the same family, danced in the same company, teach at the same ballet school, and live around the corner from each other now. Thank you for being by my side, truly, and always with love.